I WAS A NAVY AMPHIB

(APAs IN ACTION IN THE GREATEST WAR IN AMERICAN HISTORY)

Bill and Ann Stein

PublishAmerica
Baltimore

First printing

ISBN: 1-4137-6435-5
PUBLISHED BY PUBLISHAMERICA, LLLP
www.publishamerica.com
Baltimore

Printed in the United States of America

This narrative is dedicated to all the men who served in World War II, who fought so valiantly to keep our country free and to make it the greatest country in the world.

ACKNOWLEDGMENTS:

Our deepest gratitude to Higgins Industries, which provided the design for the unique landing craft used primarily in the invasions in World War II, allowing more of our men to come home safely.

Our appreciation to the Navy Department History of the USS *Clay*, APA 39, the USS *Elizabeth C. Stanton*, PA 69 and to the navy photographers who provided the pictures of war included at the end of our story.

Many thanks to our family, who encouraged us to tell the story about the courageous amphibs and their tireless contribution.

INTRODUCTION

The Navy Amphibious Force—Division L.
A special part of the enlisted men's Navy
in the greatest war in American History—
highlighting the extraordinary teamwork
of the Amphibious Force.

Early in 1942, the Amphibious Force, Atlantic Fleet, was established with a training center at Little Creek, Virginia, with a construction program for over ten thousand crafts to be completed by April, along with all the other shipbuilding demands.

Amphibious armadas were made up of many types of landing craft; LSD (landing craft dock), LCVP (landing craft personnel), LCPR (landing craft ramp), LCVM (mechanized heavy equipment), LCT (landing craft tank), and LCI-1 (infantry), etc.

Covering two oceans, the Amphibious Force carried the manpower and tools on APAs (Assault Personnel Amphibious) to all zones of war. The navy enlisted men were chosen for their special abilities. After intense physical conditioning, they were sent to schools for basic training. Specialization included seamanship, piloting, navigation, gunnery, communication, and recognition of ships and aircraft.

They underwent training courses with the Army, Navy, and Marines to learn different methods and signals in a concerted effort of cooperation. This spirit of cooperation blended the branches of service as never before in history.

Their training schooled them to properly load all types of cargo for ships and transport, how to master the cargo net to descend and climb with the rise and fall of the surf, and how to repair, land and unload while under fire—all with maximum speed to minimize the number of casualties.

Troops and supplies were transported long distance on amphibious assault vessels and put ashore in small landing boats, which the transports carried on their decks.

Each craft was manned by a coxswain (steersman), motor machinist mate (engineer), signalman (communications), and a seaman (boat hook). At the time of invasion landings, crafts from the transports were accompanied by a signal craft and an officer. They would make trip after trip, working swiftly day and night without a break until everyone and everything was unloaded at the planned destination.

A small journal found in the bottom of a sea bag inspired the following story of one sailor's amphibious experience aboard three attack transports: USS *Elizabeth C. Stanton*, USS *Clay*, and the USS *Knox*, thru the years 1942-1945, from Little Creek, Virginia, to Tokyo, Japan.

His story, as it was told, is not a history, but an actual historical picture through the eyes of one who was there. The dates and places recorded in his tiny journal refreshed his memory and allowed him to return his mind to the staggering mayhem and bitterness of war.

At the request of our two daughters, Ginny McGirk and Marlene Zamora, we have recorded some of his experiences into print.

A diary opened the doors of the mind, and the following story evolved. Excerpts from this diary are highlighted by quotation marks to separate the facts of the day from the memories.

"Oct. 2, 1942—Philadelphia Navy Yard Receiving Station."

My life changed after I drove to Philadelphia to enlist in the Navy. While at the recruiting station, I was told to go back to work and wait for a letter of acceptance. I was now concerned that the letter would not arrive before my "greeting" from Uncle Sam to serve in the Army.

My acceptance in the Navy arrived just two days before Uncle Sam's letter, and I was given instructions to report to the U.S. Customs Building, Philadelphia, Pennsylvania, no later than October 2, 1942. I had been determined to enlist in the Navy, for I was currently employed at the Washington Navy Yard in Washington, D.C. However, Wenonah, New Jersey, was my hometown and it was there that I wanted to enlist.

My dad and I drove to Philadelphia in his blue Chevy; he always liked blue. He left me off on the steps of the U.S. Customs building. The room was filled with young navy recruits, who had probably also signed up early. They all looked as scared and lonesome as I was, but I felt a little more comfortable when I saw Dan, a friend from school. He had enlisted in the Marines and had taken the elevator to the 5th floor. After a short swearing in ceremony, we boarded buses for the receiving station at the Philadelphia Navy Yard.

We all lined up while they issued us our navy uniforms, and piled our arms high with mattresses, underwear, socks, summer whites, winter blues, p-jackets, blue hats, white hats, and work dungarees. The uniforms seemed to come in two sizes, too large and too small, and it was a small miracle that they managed to find my size twelve shoes. I was not a very happy person when they plastered black stencils on everything from hats to mattress covers. The tailors did an excellent job sewing the fireman first class insignia on the sleeve of my uniform … something to be happy about.

After receiving the necessary shots, involving both arms, which started swelling immediately, we were assigned two-tiered cots and a locker in a brand new barracks. My bunk was in a corner, with two big windows to view the action in the yard. While we settled in, we were instructed how to fold our uniforms in our sea bags so they would all fit and not be wrinkled.

We were assembled and told that our group was especially chosen for the new Amphibious Force, and would be trained to man small landing boats. I soon understood that they meant small landing craft 36 feet long with 225 HP diesel engines. But, before we could go sailing into the sunset, there was to be a lot of training and naval rules and regulations to learn.

Our work duties were posted every day, and we all had to take our turns for fire watch. Our first posted duty was a work party to Fort Mifflin. We boarded a bus and traveled down the Delaware to marine quarters. The marine cooks served us a super family breakfast; there were large platters of ham and eggs, coffee, toast, orange juice and sweet rolls. After that sumptuous meal I thought, *This Navy is not so bad.*

Then, before we could relax, we were given scrapers and buckets and led to a barnacle-laden buoy and rusted chains. By lunchtime, we were covered with paint chips and rusty streaks on our new work clothes. Lunch in the marine's dining room was equally as grand as the breakfast, and it made the menial job of scraping somewhat less miserable.

That night back at the navy barracks, we were given identity badges and told that our nights were our own, but to be back to our barracks by eight in the morning. Again, I thought, *This Navy is getting better ... we were free*! By ten we were all so tired, we were glad to be back in our bunks. On the weekend, I took the ferry across the river and caught the bus home to see the folks.

Our new assignments were slow to arrive, so they gave us duty at the post-exchange. This was a lot better than scraping paint, and sometimes when we carried the groceries for the officer's wives, we got a welcome tip. I guess the chief storekeeper liked my style, for he asked for me to be his regular assignment. I was tall and helped in the warehouse stocking shelves and learned a little bit about store keeping. I soon found I was able to buy coffee, and butter, and often cigarettes. They were welcome at home for these items were hard to find and they required a ration coupon. I was glad to take them something, for they had to use their coupons for me on weekends.

In the evenings, it seemed the whole navy barracks converged on the USO, and the Stage Door Canteen. There was a lot of excitement and a big crush when the buses arrived with the girls from around the area. We had a lot of competition from the Brits for the USO girls. A British ship was in the dry dock for repairs, and their sailors made quite a splash with their wide bell-bottom pants and large blue sailor collars. There were several fights over the girls, but the Brits, even with their hob-nailed boots and all, were given the old heave-ho by our servicemen .

Several evenings I was posted for shore patrol duty, and I saw the seamier side of navy liberties. I had little trouble, for I was tall, and with snow-white leggings, the wide webbed belt, 45 automatic, night stick, shore patrol arm band and helmet, I thought I was quite an awesome sight. The night was spent stopping fights, and loading the poor, tipsy sailors into the jeep for a trip back to the ship or barracks.

With the hordes of servicemen, there were not many dancing partners available. I had a new buddy, Billy, and we met three Italian sisters, who were good dancers. Billy was single and on the prowl for girls, but I was an old married man of almost a month, and I just liked to dance. He was from Philadelphia and kept his Packard convertible, a gift from his father, at the base.

I met my wife Ann about four years ago at a ball game, where I played outfield. She was sitting in the bleachers with her sister, who was the wife of the team sponsor.

I guess you could call it one of life's memorable moments. I had just made a great play (so I thought), and slashed my knee sliding into home plate. A little slip of a girl with her long brown hair, blowing in the wind, was sitting on the end bench cheering for the team. She glanced my way and I expected her to say what a great play I had made, but she said: "Why aren't you more careful? You've got sand spurs all over your new uniform."

I still marvel at my quick-witted repartee: I answered, "I know. Do you want to pick them off?"

Now you know how it all started. Ann came to Wenonah from Alexandria, Virginia, to visit her sister on holidays and vacations. When she left we wrote long letters and exchanged song sheets each week. Ann taught me to dance, and her sister did not complain about the wear and tear on her rug. Ann had learned Arthur Murray's rumba, fox trot and swing, and I really enjoyed it even with my size twelve feet.

My best buddy Bill Allen, who was Ann's friend too, had an old Chevy, and on Sundays we all piled in and headed for Atlantic City. The best bands came to the Steel Pier, and we danced the night away; and then it was the moon, boardwalk, and saltwater taffy.

After graduation, I worked at Kruse and Slattery's machine shop in Camden for fifty cents an hour. Thinking of the future, I considered the security and benefits of a government job, so Ann sent me forms for employment at the Washington Navy Yard in D.C. I passed the test and was soon attending machinist school, with hands-on work in the ordinance section. The best part of all, I was getting paid.

One day our shop foreman announced that he had a special assignment for us outside the Navy Yard. We were boarded on trucks and taken to assemble and mount anti-aircraft guns on top of the old torpedo plant on the Potomac River in Alexandria, Virginia. After we finished, we crossed the river to Andrews Air Force Base and assembled more guns. Our work hours often extended far into the night, and with winches and cranes, we assembled and mounted anti-aircraft 1.1s on top of the highest rooftops and on the roofs of the Departments of War. Everything was accomplished with the highest amount of secrecy possible. The Army was also billeted on the roofs, trained and ready. It looked like the war was coming right to our doorstep.

Our shop received a model of the Swedish Bofer 40 mm anti-aircraft gun with twin and quad mounts. We assembled it for display and there was a hurried clean-up detail when it was announced that Frank Knox, the Secretary of the Navy, was going to inspect this new weapon.

This 40 mm weapon was badly needed to replace the old 1.1s. Our transports and other ships of war needed more gun power and speedier response to defend us from the tenacious enemy aircraft attacks.

When Pearl Harbor was bombed on December 7, 1941, very few people even knew where Pearl Harbor was, but when President Roosevelt spoke on the radio, it soon became known in every household. Ann was working in the accounting department of Julius Garfinkle & Co. when the Navy Department put out a call for help for employees in the department. Ann joined the ranks of office girls who invaded Washington, D.C. for the duration. At least Ann had her family home to return to at night, while the girls from across the country were crammed in the many boarding houses in the area.

I rented a little room in Alexandria, number 8 Alexandria Avenue, to be exact. I picked Ann up from work and we spent evenings together, and on weekends we were with her family or headed to New Jersey in my Chevy coupe, which needed a bucket of water every fifty miles or so.

The war draft hung heavily over our heads, for I was 1-A, and in good health. My draft number could be called at any time. I requested a job release from the Navy Yard, but Bill, our shop's master mechanic, said no, absolutely not, the Navy Yard was giving no deferments! To them making guns was just as important as firing them. My best buddy Bill Allen had finished basic training, and our friend Dave was still in college waiting for his call from Uncle Sam. I had already been taunted about why I was not in uniform, so with several others, I went to Captain Palmer's office and got a release.

Ann and I were both in shock; we could not believe what was happening to our lives. I had given her an engagement ring about a year ago, and we were making serious plans. When reality finally set in I asked her the question. "You will wait for me won't you?"

I noticed she shook her head "no" even before she answered. "We have known each other for four years, and after separations we are back together again. You may now be gone for a whole year, possibly longer. There will be many things to tear us apart, and a wedding ring may not be a guarantee, but we need an anchor to give us some meaning to our future. If you do not feel the same, it is best we part now as friends, for any path we choose right now will determine our whole life."

Ann was 21, but I would not be 21 until February. We got our blood test and traveled to Fairfax Court House for our license. She was small and they asked to see her birth certificate, but they did not even question me. I guess they thought if I was big enough, I was old enough.

Ann's father was bedridden from a severe coronary attack and very weak, so we went alone to the Presbyterian Church in Alexandria on St. Asaph Street. At high noon on September 28, 1942, we became Mr. and Mrs. William Charles Stein. The church bells tolled and the firehouse whistle announced the noon of day, (and our wedding), with no one to see but God and the preacher. My folks in New Jersey had to be told, so we went next door to the post office, and on a paper bag, we wrote the good news and sent our announcement.

We packed our little Chevy, and an extra can of water, and were off to the Shenandoah Valley for our glorious three-day honeymoon. The trees on the Blue Ridges were a riot of fall colors, as we strolled hand in hand through the Natural Bridge and Jefferson's interesting home at Monticello, trying not to think of the future. One thing was certain, even though we were a little sad and afraid of our uncertain future; we were married, on a nice honeymoon and had the pictures to show for it.

Back at the barracks in Philadelphia, the wheels of the Navy moved slowly. Ann came up to Wenonah on weekends, and we had two days together. On Sunday night I'd go back to the barracks and she took the train, loaded with servicemen, back to Washington, D.C.

Christmas was the saddest day yet. I had a gut feeling that everything was about to change. Ann came up from Virginia, and I couldn't wait to give her the little gold watch I had been saving up to buy for her. I guess time was on our minds, for Dad gave me a watch also. It was something quite new … it was waterproof! The face was black and the gold numbers would glow in the dark. He remarked that it was just the thing for the Navy, and I silently hoped I would not be dunking it in the water, at least not right away. I made use of my dad's camera and took pictures of the folks in the yard, and they took pictures of Ann and me in my new uniform, and our new watches.

New Year's Eve and we were still in Philadelphia. With nothing better to do, we went downtown to see the sights. Servicemen were everywhere. There was scarcely room on the sidewalks, and our hopes of getting served at a restaurant evaporated, so we settled for a movie, and immediately fell asleep. What a night.

There was a bit of excitement when the posted orders for the day were snow-white leggings and dress winter blues. The great battleship *New Jersey* was to be christened at the Yard. We all gave our best salute as the newest ship of war slid down and splashed into the Delaware River. As she eased out into the river, a giant suction removed all the water from the slip and a back wave washed into the area, showering us all as we scrambled for higher elevation.

Sadly, the horrors of war came right to the Navy Yard. The wounded Boise limped into the dry dock for major repairs. We were all sobered by the hushed rumor that after her last Pacific battle, bodies were still contained in the hold, and needed to be retrieved. Her number one turret had been damaged, and there were casualties from the magazine explosion.

January was almost over, and we were biding our time when orders were posted that we would be shipping out on January 22. For once I was first in line at the phones, and Ann was soon on her way to Wenonah.

"THUR. JAN 21, 1943 SPENT LAST NIGHT WITH THE FOLKS, ANN CAME UP FROM VIRGINIA."

Mother served a terrific meal, as usual, and we just sat quietly, each thinking about what the future would hold. I had that sick feeling in my stomach, and I'm sure Ann felt the same. Dad kept swallowing and clearing his throat. Mother tried to joke and said, "Well, kid, now that you are in the Navy, you won't have to eat Saturday slop any more." It was an old joke we had at home about Saturday leftovers. She had always called me kid and I called her Mother. My birth mother died of tuberculosis when I was only a year and a half old. My dad, broken hearted and left with a small child, moved back with his parents and sisters to Audubon, New Jersey.

Victor Talking Machine Company started their first recording company in Camden, New Jersey, and Dad was their first arranger and recorder. Having been a machinist at the Navy Yard, and an accomplished flutist with the Philadelphia Orchestra, he combined his talents to grind diamond-recording needles. A diamond needle is extremely hard and long lasting, and because of the value of the gem, he was locked in a vault during the process. Lawrence Tibbitt, Paul Whitman and many orchestra leaders sent him letters of praise for the balance and clarity of his recordings. He was sent to Japan for one year, to make recordings of Japanese music and opera singers, leaving his six-year-old behind. When Radio Corporation of America bought out the Victor Company, Dad was eased out, and I don't think he ever quite recovered, for recording had become a large part of his life. He returned from Japan when I was seven and married Mary. As a stepmother, she did everything for me to make up for the loss of my mother. I know I gave her a hard time growing up, but she was such a fine woman, I thank God I never let her down.

My last night with the folks and Ann passed in a flash and I was up before dawn for the trip back to the barracks. Mother insisted I have bacon and eggs, and I remember her saying, "Kid, take care of yourself." It was still dark when I left, and Ann put on my pajama top, and they went back to bed. I caught the bus at the corner, and it took every ounce of courage to not leave the bus at the next stop and go home.

"Fri. Jan. 22, 1943 Left Philadelphia Navy Yard for Portsmouth, Va. Arrived there at 8 P.M."

It was doom and gloom on the train ride to Portsmouth, and the clicking of the wheels kept saying *to what, to where*. There was a bus waiting to take us to the naval receiving station, and to our assigned barracks. Again they gave us a Navy haircut and short arm inspection. I don't know why, we had not been near any women since our last inspection. For the next few days it was exercise and drills, and drills and exercise.

"Mon. Jan. 25, 1943 Left Portsmouth, Va. for Solomons, Md."

On January 25, we boarded a barge-type ferry. There was a huge room below, and we got our mattresses from the sea bags and tried to sleep. The noise from the engine, and the cold rusty deck provided little comfort. When it was announced that we were going to Solomons Island, I could only think of the one in the Pacific. Surely, we would not be going to sea in this junker.

The motor thumped and bumped as we left the Chesapeake Bay and chugged up the Patuxent River. I knew then that we were not going to sea.

"Tues. Jan. 26, 1943 Arrived at Solomons, Md. Amphibious Training Base."

We had a poor night's sleep and by now the rain had turned to snow and sleet. Everything was covered with a thin sheet of ice and the mud was frozen in big ruts where the trucks had passed. We slipped and slid trying to get our footing up the sloping path to the mess hall. We stayed at the base five miserable days, just having meals and trying to keep warm and dry.

"Sun. Jan. 31, 1943 Left Solomons Isl. Md. for Little Creek Amphibious Training Base in Virginia. Arrived at 10 P.M. Tomorrow is Mother's birthday."

The old LST they put us on had a cavernous tank deck, which was our sleeping place. It was cold … cold as only a steel bed can be in winter. We had been in the dark so long we thought it was morning when the LST pulled up at the base. Groggy and hoping for a warmer bed, we were informed that our records were lost and we could not check in until new records were made. We lined up for more shots, in both arms again, stripped for another health exam, and waited while they printed up new dog tags. I felt like a dog—wet, hungry, and cold.

To add insult to injury, the mess hall was closed and the leftover cold creamed potatoes and onions did little to warm us up. This was just the beginning of the many times I would wish for Mother's Saturday slop.

We sloshed around in about six inches of snow and it was still snowing. We had been assigned a Quonset hut number, but it was dark, as only a blackout can be. Finally, with the feeble help of someone's cigarette lighter, we found the Quonset hut (of our dreams), and I noticed it was one-thirty A.M., by my new watch.

To say there was a lot of cussing going on would be putting it mildly, for our cots were still in a bundle and the kerosene heaters were out of oil. Hasty assignments were made, and we were finally ready to bunk in.

I had the first watch, and I filled all the oil heaters and made the security checks, then I bunked down for heavenly sleep at last.

About five o'clock in the morning, I woke up shivering and cold to the bone. For a few seconds I couldn't figure out where I was, and then we all got up and found the culprit who had missed his fire watch duty, and dumped him out of his cot. On our way to the mess hall in the morning, navy sea bags were piled up outside covered with snow, looking like drunken snowmen. Hungry new recruits who had their fill of the cold and the navy shuffle would soon find that the navy brig was no improvement.

About two nights later, the same clod who had missed his fire watch duty came in the hut about 3:00 A.M. He was returning from a pass to town, and was so bombed he passed out as soon as his head hit the cot. There was to be no rest for us. His snoring was so horrendous and the odor from the sour whisky so overwhelming, we finally had to take matters into our own hands.

He continued to snore as we lifted the cot and placed it out in the snow. Early the next morning, bare footed and wrapped in his blanket like a squaw, he sought the warmth of the Quonset hut. There were no more late nights or shirking of the fire watch duty.

The mess hall and recreation areas were about a half mile away. We were issued slickers (weather still bad), and taken on night hikes up the beach to Ocean Park and returned to the base by the back roads. When we worked with our landing craft, everything was freezing and the sea spray had us all soaked to the skin, even with our rain gear. It was a hopeless task to try to practice our V formation landings, for the force of the wind left many disabled.

I was concerned about my friend Bill; he had missed a roll call, and was AWOL. The next day, he was back at the base, big as life and not too concerned. He had gone to Philadelphia for his Packard, and his latest girl friend. I did not know if he was reprimanded or not, but I guess his dad would have patched things up for him.

"Sat. Feb. 6, 1943 Went on weekend liberty in Alex. to see Ann, got in Alex. at 9:15 P.M."

It would have been nice to have my car in Alexandria, but with the Washington traffic and gas rationing, we decided to leave it in Dad's garage in New Jersey. Ann did not want the responsibility or the expense. Her father was still not able to get around much, and he agonized over the war news. Gabriel Heater's news commentary, about the German wolf packs covering the Atlantic, kept us all worried and on edge. Each day more and more American ships were being sunk, and we seemed helpless to defend our convoys.

The weekend at Ann's house did not give us much privacy with her mom and dad, and two older brothers, so we borrowed the family car and took a little ride down the Mount Vernon Boulevard to watch the boats on the Potomac River.

All we wanted was to be alone; we had only been married a little over four months, and together just a few days total. Just to be together and to hold each other was a treat, and we tried to pretend there was no tomorrow parting.

Lost in the euphoria of the moment, we were startled by lights flashing in our eyes. A burley park policeman tapped on the window and said, "You lovers get along home." I tried to explain our situation, but he told us rules are rules; and no parking after dark.

"Sun. Feb. 7, 1943 Left for Little Creek 7 P.M. from Washington, D.C."

Ann went with me to Union Station. Servicemen and women were all on the move to somewhere, saying goodbyes and trying to keep warm on the drafty boarding platforms. The car on the train was filled, and some were sitting on their bags. There was no heat, but I dozed part of the way leaning on the back of a seat. All of the returning servicemen seem to have had a sobering weekend for the car was unusually silent. I heard a few murmuring voices discussing their orders to ship out to San Francisco the following week.

"Mon. Feb. 8, 1943 Reached Little Creek 3 A.M."

"Tues. Feb. 16, 1943—21 years old today."

We had calisthenics and marching drill in the morning, afternoon and evening. That time of year, the days were short and it would get dark early. The instructor couldn't see us in the dark, so we would slip away unnoticed and get a little rest. I think they were trying to kill us. When we were not exercising or marching, we studied the navy manual, ship identification and codes of communication.

"Sat. March 13, 1943 Left Little Creek for Amphibious Training Base at Ft. Pierce, Fla. at 7 P.M. Got traveling bag and ring from Ann."

Ann mailed me a black traveling bag, which I needed. She also sent me a box with a wedding band in it. She said she was not taking any chances; it was protection from all the girls at the USO. I wrote and told her not to worry; I had a bad feeling that where I was headed, there would be no girls, or USO.

There was a lot of activity, and I was sure that we were about to be on the move again. The announcement was posted; we were leaving for Fort Pierce, Florida, at 7 P.M. Our training with the landing had been difficult, with the cold and ice causing delays. I had never been to Florida, but it had to be warmer than the Chesapeake Bay in February.

We were getting used to train hopping by now and made the best of it. When we made our first big stop in Jacksonville, I slipped into a nearby store and bought Ann the largest card I could find. It had two big red satin hearts on the front with the words, "Love to my wife, from her husband in the service."

When we boarded the train, it was time for dinner … beans and franks again. After a long wait, we finally left the dining car to be greeted by a clanking and swooshing noise. We got to the observation platform just in time to see the train had become uncoupled and the cars were already fading from sight. Like in an old movie, we all rushed to pull the emergency cord. The engineer backed up about two miles, which brought cheers from the passengers left behind.

"SUN. MARCH 14, 1943 ARRIVED IN FT. PIERCE AT 11 P.M., 28-HOUR TRIP."

I could not believe the change in the weather. It was like Shangri-La from the movie; freezing snow and cold, then paradise. The moon was out, casting its shadows through the waving palms and pine trees.

Army ducks met us at the train station. They were so high up from the ground that we joked that we needed a cargo net to get aboard. They drove us over a narrow, clanky bridge, which crossed the inter-coastal to Fort Pierce Island.

Lucky, lucky us, we went from Quonset huts to a small tent city. At least the floor and sides were wooden and off the sand, which was infested with mosquitoes and sand crabs. As far as we could tell, there was nothing there but sand dunes, pine trees, and a jungle of palmettos.

The following day, the fare did not get any more luxurious. Our "mess" hall consisted of boards, six inches wide, nailed between two pine trees. The tin mess kits we were issued did not fit on the board, and we had to use one hand to keep it from falling. We soon found out that the large drum of water at the end of our dining "table" was waiting for us to dunk our dirty dishes, then to dry them in the sea breeze. There was no time to linger at our dining, for our intensive training was about to start. We spent part of the day with vigorous calisthenics, and then were introduced to our area of practice.

At the inlet, there was a mock-up of a ship to practice with, and then the blistering days of work began. The Atlantic surf was very high, and our first attempts to maneuver our crafts were sorry indeed. We slammed into the mock-up, got broached, flooded out and stalled. We needed a lot more practice siding up to the ship's cargo net in the heavy surf and holding it tight to board the troops, and practice we did. Landings on the beaches were equally as tricky. One false move and the water could fly up the lowered ramp like a flume and turn the craft on its side. We could drown the engines, or the men, who were loaded with heavy equipment, or even worse, make them targets for the enemy.

The sand dunes on the beach were piled up with machine gun placements, and we practiced being the enemy and the attackers. The inlet was quite narrow, but we rehearsed the circle pattern of loading troops so that all craft could be loaded and proceed with the landings all together in a giant V formation. We often worked long after dark, and were so tired we could not do much more than flop into our cots, letting the balmy sea breeze caress our aching bones. I met two guys from New Jersey; Frankie, who lived south of my folks and another Frankie, who lived near Pitman. Both were married with young wives like mine.

"Sun. March 28, 1943 Married six months today. Haven't had much time to enjoy it."

I thought I was in great shape when I joined the Navy. I had participated in boxing at school, was a runner and ran everywhere I went. On weekends I rode my bicycle often thirty or more miles, and was on a softball team. The new regiment in the amphibious training left me muscle lean and brown from the Florida sun. After two weeks I was lifting barrels of fuel like sofa pillows.

The nightly news gave us the latest information about the war, but the stark reality was on our doorstep. Commentators reported the disastrous action of the German U-boats on our shipping and transports. Here we saw the horrible proof; our beach was littered with wreckage floating in with the tide. Before we could launch our boats, we would collect personal belongings, rotting food, dead fish, and sometimes body parts. Even the inlet had its hazards ... grapefruit, oranges, coconut shells, and rotting bananas.

The debris of war was quite unnerving, for we knew the U-boat U128 had attacked and sunk the tanker Pan Massachusetts in early February. The location had been forty miles south east of Cape Canaveral, not too far north of our location. Two more ships were sunk later in February. The German wolf packs were like piranhas on the prowl, and we watched with apprehension as the fires of torpedoed ships flared on the horizon.

Scuttlebutt news was out that we would be staying in Florida about a month. I finally got a call through to Ann at work, but she had been sent to the main navy building with some contracts. Her supervisor was so concerned when she learned I was in Florida, she took my message and started a request for Ann's leave of absence to go to Fort Pierce. The Navy Department was lenient with navy wives, especially when their husbands were in the States.

"THU. APRIL 1, 1943 TOMORROW IS DAD'S BIRTHDAY."

"FRI. APRIL 2, 1943 ANN ARRIVED IN FT. PIERCE AT 5 P.M., 10TH WEEK IN THE NAVY. SURE GLAD TO SEE HER."

Annie was a sight for sore eyes as she stepped from the Tami-Ami Special dressed in her little hat and white gloves. The Taylor Hotel was not far and we checked in and went to dinner at Johnnie's Café. My friend Frankie's wife Esther was already in Fort Pierce and we saw them in the dining room. Esther was quite small with short blonde hair and very pale. Frankie explained to me that Esther had just lost a baby, and he hoped the Florida sunshine would cheer her up a bit. We talked a while and made arrangements to take a trip to Palm Beach. A short train trip south would bring us back by nighttime. We wondered what the girls would do all day, and we found a little park in back of the hotel where there were benches and palm trees. The hedges about the hotel and park were red hibiscus, and bright blooms were everywhere. They tried to get a Florida tan on the sand at the edge of the coastal river, but the pelicans were so thick, keeping them away was more work than pleasure.

"SAT. APRIL 3, 1943 GOT A 48-HR. LIBERTY AND WENT TO PALM BEACH WITH ANN. HAD A SWELL TIME."

A 48-hour pass, I was on cloud nine. The weather was great, and we had breakfast at the same restaurant. Every meal, every order was preceded by a stainless steel compote of orange and grapefruit cocktail. We did not have a shortage of citrus, for a big packing plant was just by the bridge to our island. Luckily the guards were looking away when we slid an orange or two from the packing cases when we passed. Ann kept a supply of citrus on the windowsill of the hotel.

The train trip to Palm Beach seemed short, especially since we were finally on a train trip together. A first trip to Florida has a special magic. You are now doing the things you have read or heard about in songs or in the movies. The day was like being in a wonderland, warm sand and palm trees gently blowing in the tropical breeze. Frankie and Esther warmed up to our company, and the pictures we took that day kept the special moments in our memory.

"SUN. APRIL 4, 1943 SPENT THE DAY IN FT. PIERCE WITH ANN. HAD DINNER AND WENT TO A SHOW WITH FRANKIE AND ESTHER."

Frankie and Esther were from a town just below Wenonah, and Esther lived on a farm with her parents while she was recuperating from the loss of her baby. We wanted to cheer her up so we asked them to go to a movie on the base. The movie house was an old wooden structure with bleacher seats, but we were happy just to be together. The movie had just begun when a bulletin flashed on the screen for all military personnel to report immediately back to the base of operations.

There was a mad rush for the exits, and the girls were on their own to return to the hotel. The next evening we explained our hasty exit. A small German submarine had been sighted by a volunteer observer. Apparently, the Germans had put personnel ashore in our area. We were issued 45 automatics and assigned patrols to search the island and the surrounding areas. We saw a fire burning a short distance off shore, and a lot of debris was washing in with the tide. We wondered what ship the broken gangway and charred rafts had come from. Our area was searched until dawn, and we knew they were not in our immediate vicinity. We never heard if anyone was apprehended; I don't suppose they would have told us anyway.

"Mon. April 5, 1943 Got special overnight liberty to spend with Ann."

No one had to tell us how important our training had become. We trained with a determined vigor, and were dead tired at the end of the day. When I got a special overnight liberty, I forgot about my aching muscles, and jogged all the way to the hotel. Everything felt right, like this paradise was going to last forever; like a dream you don't want to wake up from.

"Tues. April 6, 1943 Ditto."

My dream did last for a few more days. My ensign was also from New Jersey, and he made sure I had a liberty pass every night while Ann was here. What a great guy.

"Wed. April 7, 1943 Ditto."

"Thu. April 8, 1943 Ditto."

"Fri. April 9, 1943 Ditto."

"Sat. April 10, 1943 Danced a while at Johnnie's Café with Ann."

"Sun. April 11, 1943 Ann's last day in Ft. Pierce. Saw a picture show, *Forever and a Day.* Took two rolls of film."

I never saw time fly so fast. The last ten days were like a paradise vacation. The little park in back of the hotel was a nice place to take pictures. We posed under the royal palm and sat on the benches and the cute little bridge. The sick feeling in my stomach, which had been hiding for a few days, returned, for I knew Ann would soon be leaving and I would be shipping out for somewhere shortly. On our last night together we did not see much of the movie *Forever and a Day*, and I hoped the title wasn't a prediction of how long I would be gone.

Thankfully, there were not any messages on the screen for a recall to the base, and our last night together was not interrupted.

"MON. APRIL 12, 1943 SAID SO LONG TO ANN THIS MORNING AT 6 A.M. ANN LEFT FT. PIERCE TODAY FOR HOME. MISS HER A LOT."

After Ann boarded the train, I gave a silent goodbye to the Taylor Hotel, our temporary home for ten days. Now it was back to the base and the grueling amphibious rehearsals. We were training for night landings, communicating with small blue-hooded flashlights. We ate and slept when we could get the chance, always pushing the clock to the limit.

"MON. APRIL 12, 1943 ANN'S STORY."

(Meanwhile, Ann was speeding toward Virginia on the Orange Blossom Special.)

The aisles were packed with sea bags, duffel bags and suitcases, as another Navy wife and I worked our way through the coaches. We found an area to stand when a young private offered us his seat. We were about the only women on the train and we got a warm welcome, to say the least. There was not much room for luggage, but we found a safe place and headed for the dining car. The line was backed up through the train to the lounge car, and we could hardly move. The car was filled with wounded servicemen being transported from the hospital in Miami for rehabilitation. There were walking wounded in every seat and couch, and some of the wounded were seated on the floor. The food line did not move for some time, and a soldier bedded on the couch slid his crutches to one side to give me an edge to sit on. I took the pillow he had been lying on and put it on my lap for him to rest his head. I could see that his head had been shaved and a large dressing was taped at the area over his ear. A larger bandage was wound around his head to keep the dressing in place. There was a pillow under his foot, and I could see a canvas-type brace up as far as his knee. The area below his ankle was covered with a blanket. I wondered if he had lost a foot. It had taken quite an effort for him to make room for me and I could see he was visibly shaken.

By the time the line had moved up, the soldier was sound asleep. I tried to slip from the couch, but every time I tried to move him he started moaning and moving his head from side to side. I finally calmed him down but decided that I would have to look for some food very soon. Before I could act on my decision, the cook entered the car with a tray of sandwiches and a pot of coffee; at least I wouldn't starve. The soldier seemed woozy and I helped him with his drink. (I think he exaggerated a little.) Again I started to leave and he asked me to please stay. I settled down to what became a long night, for he was instantly asleep again.

The girl who was traveling with me came by with a navy chief in tow. She told me she was going to get her bag and stay the night in the chief's coach. When she offered to bring my suitcase to me, I was relieved for I was worried about my luggage. Sleep came and went through interruptions and noise. At least the couch was softer than the straight coach seat. I was very cramped and worried about the condition of my dress. At one point he aroused and talked about his girl friend back home, but most of the time he tossed and turned. I smoothed his hair, and searched his youthful, pain-creased face. Would this be the fate of my Bill, who was about to be sent to who knows where? All sorts of horrors flashed through my mind; would his beautiful, strong body be maimed also? I could still visualize the first time we met. His hair was curly and damp from the exertion of the ball game and my heart tripped at that Gary Cooper smile as he said his first words to me. The wounded soldier on my lap moaned in his sleep, and I tried to make him more comfortable. Most of the boys in the coach had been wounded in Africa and had the insignia on their uniforms of an armored division.

I had to leave him on the couch when the train arrived at Union Station in D.C. and he asked me to kiss him goodbye, which I did. He was crying a little and I did not look back … he seemed so young.

After my Florida paradise, it was difficult to return to work, but the next morning I was up at 6 A.M. to catch the bus for Washington. The Navy Department was bustling with its usual wartime activity, and for me, more days ahead worrying and praying for the safe return of the man in my life.

End of Ann's Story

"SUN. APRIL 25, 1943 EASTER, WENT TO CHURCH SERVICE AT CAMP."

Easter Sunday was a welcome day of rest. We attended the camp service in the morning, and lounged in our bunks reading the manual or just reading letters. Most of us fell asleep. The sudden inactivity was like the lull before a storm. We had been gearing up all week, and I felt sure we would soon be on the move. I felt especially fortunate that Ann had been able to spend time with me at the base. It had been so hard to say goodbye again. Oh lonesome me!

"MON. APRIL 26, 1943 LEFT FT. PIERCE, FLA. FOR VIRGINIA AT 1:00 P.M. STOPPED IN JACKSONVILLE FROM 8:00-11:00 P.M."

Another train trip, back to Norfolk again, and I felt like a seasoned traveler. I had never been on a train before, and now I had made several trips in seven months. The trip took a boring thirty-one hours and there was little to do except read or play cards, and I was never a great card player. We were all so young, the government had not taught us to smoke or drink … yet.

"TUES. APRIL 27, 1943 ARRIVED IN NORFOLK NAVAL BASE RECEIVING STATION AT 8 P.M. GOT TO AMPHIBIOUS TRAINING BASE AT CAMP BRADFORD, VA. AT 12 P.M."

I assumed that the base at Norfolk was not quite ready for us, so they loaded us on buses and shipped us to Camp Bradford for holding.

What joy, another tent city. However, we were close to Norfolk and they let us have a few liberties while we were waiting for orders.

"WED. APRIL 28, 1943 CALLED ANN ON LIBERTY IN NORFOLK—MARRIED 7 MONTHS TODAY."

"SAT. MAY 1, 1943 BOARDED U.S.S. *ELIZABETH C. STANTON* AT NORFOLK, VA., HAMPTON ROADS."

We left the tent city at Camp Bradford behind and boarded the bus for Hampton Roads. There she was, the U.S.S. *Elizabeth C. Stanton*, looking larger to me than the Empire State Building. It seemed more mountainous as the small motorboats neared her gangway, with the amphibious division plus their pile of sea bags aboard. The *Lizzie*, as we learned to call her, was rocking at anchor, and I felt a sense of pride and belonging. We were finally, actually on a ship and we all were thankful for our training. I saluted the flag smartly and also the officers of the deck. The commander of the amphibious task force had already reported aboard to make ready for our various drills and exercises. A salty mate escorted us to a small compartment forward, next to #2 hold. There were about twenty men in our group, and we slept in bunks four high.

The ship had seen service in the merchant marine and had been overhauled and converted to a transport. Our private mess hall was comfortable with wooden tables and benches. So far the food was good. The large wooden table had a slot down the middle and we soon learned what "butter down" meant. We made a game of shooting butter and sugar down the slot on demand. When the bosun piped the "chow down" over the loud speaker, we wasted no time getting to our mess hall.

Showers were another thing. The hours and instructions were posted. The water will be turned on 4 P.M.-6 P.M. Soap your body all over first and then rinse, turning off water in between. The only hot water available had to be caught in a bucket, as needed, so we made do with cold water most of the time. The bosun made another announcement over the speaker before we pulled anchor; all white hats must be dyed blue. The ship at sea must be in total blackout, and a white cap would be a visible target for the German U-boats. We were all directed to the deck where a large vat of blue dye was waiting for us.

The *Stanton* had been in convoy to Oran, Algiers, several times, transporting troops and supplies, and many of the ship's crew were seasoned veterans of the African invasion.

"Tues. May 4, 1943 Tried to call the folks, couldn't get through, called Ann."

We were given a short liberty, and sailors were lined up at the telephones. I finally got my turn, but I couldn't get a line through to Mother and Dad. I did get through to Ann and gave her my new address: William C. Stein Fireman, 2/c, L Division, U.S.S. *Elizabeth C. Stanton*, c/o FPO New York, N. Y.

Of course we could say nothing else about our ship movements. There were signs posted all over about, "Loose lips sink ships," and I knew we would soon be in the dangerous Atlantic. I tried to be cheerful on the phone, and since there were many waiting to place calls, I gave her a few coded messages and hung up. There was an unwelcome feeling of finality in our conversation, and I felt blue again.

"Thu. May 6, 1943 Called folks while on liberty."

I finally got a call through to Mother and Dad. There was not much I could say, just what ship I was on and that I was fine.

Our drills with a real ship were quite a bit different. The bay was a lot better than the ocean, and a little different than the mock-up at Fort Pierce. Operating our crafts next to this awesome ship gave us a preview of landings to come. Our training was now at an accelerated pace and we knew we would soon be putting all our training to use.

We were loading up and I watched with fascination the expertise of our ship's boom handlers. The huge cargo nets, loaded with supplies, were swung through the air with precision and were placed quickly and exactly in the right spot in the hold or on a waiting boat. It was an air ballet in action, and they lifted the ship's jeep like it was a feather, and placed it lightly on the upper deck. This amazing scene would be repeated over and over at the scene of every invasion before we returned to the States again.

"Sat. May 8, 1943 Left the supply depot at Norfolk for Newport News."

We were on the move. The boom handlers pulled our landing craft out of the water and placed them on the deck two high, with skids in between. A few boats were hung over the side, and several were on forward deck. Our two tank lighters were placed aft at the stern hatch. When our crafts came aboard, we were ready to sail. There was one task left; to board the troops at Newport News. There would be little room on the ship when they brought all their bags, arms and armament aboard.

Captain Ross A. Dierdorff, United States Navy, came aboard in February and was always visible on the bridge or walking the deck. He was a gentle, fatherly figure who commanded obedience and respect from his crew simply because of his many years of experience and his aura of self-confidence.

"Sun. May 9, 1943 Picked up troops. Got last letter from Ann."

We boarded the troops, with their duffel bags, guns and light armament. Every inch of the deck was covered; resembling a giant can of sardines. They were divided into groups, some doing exercises and some working on their equipment. The amphibious crew was assigned battle stations for general quarters and given our time for fire watch stations. Everyone gathered for a final mail call in the States, and I was not disappointed, for I had a letter from Ann. We all knew we would soon be leaving for Europe, and could only imagine when or where our next mail call would be.

"MON. MAY 10, 1943 LEFT NEWPORT NEWS AT 9:00 A.M. PICKED UP CONVOY AND LEFT THE STATES FOR ???"

The captain was on the bridge as we pulled anchor at the mouth of the Chesapeake Bay. Other ships were anchored out waiting for us to join the convoy of about fifty vessels. There were cargo ships, oilers, transports, destroyers, and escort vessels. Many had traveled cautiously down the coast from New York City.

The Straits of Florida, Bahamas, and the Gulf of Mexico were lucrative hunting grounds for the German submarine wolf packs. Our air and sea protection was still not fully organized, and the German U-boats had sunk 41 ships in the Gulf of Mexico in the month of May 1942 alone. Although our retaliation was swift with a squadron of Hudson bombers from Jacksonville and B25s from Miami, the attacks from the U-boats were still brazen and daring.

There was danger every day, and we practiced our general quarters station. Sometimes I was assigned the gun watch midships and the aircraft watch topside. The 20 mm anti-aircraft gun I was assigned was similar to the ones we practiced with at Fort Pierce. This particular one was a Swiss Orlicon. Guns were of special interest to me for my grandfather had been a gunsmith from Giessen Germany, and I had also worked on and assembled the Swedish Bofer 40 mm aircraft gun at the Washington Navy Yard.

Around the edges of our convoy, numbered UGF 8 A, were escort blimps. For our safety, we were traveling the interlocking convoy system. The blimps constantly watched the water for periscopes or any unknown shadows in the water. They traveled with us as far as their fuel would last; meanwhile the destroyer escorts circled the convoy communicating ship to air constantly. When the blimps turned back, the long-range reconnaissance airplanes appeared to cover the next step in the convoy's journey. They were a welcome sight, and stayed with us as far as their fuel allowed.

"Tues. May 11, 1943 One month since I last saw Ann, seems much longer."

Today I stood gun watch four hours on and four hours off. My nerves were on edge, and the stress caused a sharp pain in my neck and shoulders. Large black and red spots kept passing before my eyes as I strained to watch for anything in the water. The reflection and the heavy helmet with the ear phones gave me a bad headache, and I was glad when each watch was over. Our master of arms warned all of us, "Never take your helmet off, or your life belt, and never roll up your sleeves at general quarters. Your safety from fire, water and aircraft may depend upon these rules." We were lucky; our master of arms was a congenial cuss, always looking out for our safety. Also, if we were sound asleep, after a hard day's work, he would just tap on our bunk lightly and let us sleep a little more, as long as we met muster, or were at our battle stations on time. Between our posted assignments, our amphibious group had the navy manual to study.

Radio work was complicated, and we reviewed the codes and signals for the communications needed at the time of invasions. There were radio signals, hand signals, Morse code, plus ship identification. The coxswain was responsible for the craft's navigation; however, the engineer was trained as well and was ready and often needed for this operation. Our chores continued around the clock, and the *Stanton* was tight and well run. I felt a close kinship to her already.

"Sun. May 16, 1943 One week out today, clear weather so far, except for a few showers last Friday."

Security was tighter than ever. The reconnaissance planes were at their fuel limit and we were now very vulnerable in the water. The escorting destroyers patrolled anxiously and the zigzag pattern of the convoy kept us busy with the silent communication to attend to. We were pleased that the weather was clear and visibility at its highest point.

At this point we had complete radio silence, for this was the most dangerous part of our crossing, and we communicated with flags and flashes only.

"MON. MAY 17, 1943 STOOD CROW'S NEST 1200-1400."

At this time we were about halfway across the Atlantic headed for Africa. Our new worry now, other than U-boats, was the German pocket battleships. We were zigzagging at only 10 knots, for the old cargo ships in our convoy were slow, and of course that made us easier targets for the German submarines.

When I checked the board watch list, I noticed my name. *Stein, W.C.—Crow's nest, 1200-1400.* Were my eyes failing me? Surely, they did not mean I was to have a watch in that little box swaying at the top of the ship's mast! If I had wanted to do a high-wire act, I would have joined the circus, not the Navy.

My sparse lunch did not set well, I was so nervous. When I looked at the base of the mast, I knew why I was selected. The entrance ring at the bottom of the ladder was small, only about twenty inches wide. I was thin and tall, in fact, on the ball team at home, they called me snaky for the way I ran around the bases.

At first glance I figured I would have to remove my life belt. (No way.) If our ship was torpedoed, I would become a human cannonball in a very high dive. I would need that belt. After a stretch and a wiggle, I made it through, but after a few steps, I realized that my size twelve shoes were a definite hazard. The rail was my lifeline and I hung on for dear life. To look down would have been a disaster, and I decided to check to see if I was at the top. I was only halfway.

At that moment, the ship made a turn to the starboard, and I braced my legs against the high seas and the turning of the ship. Without any lessons at all, I was performing a ridiculous high-wire hula. When I stopped shaking, I felt a little sick, but I thought of the many soldiers on board who were sick from the rough Atlantic, and I was thankful for my strong stomach, especially right now.

At last, the top of the mast and another hazard. The hatch at the top was so small, I barely fit. The earphones, which connected to the bridge and all gun stations, and the binoculars, were hanging on a hook as the bosun had instructed me. I carefully unhooked the safety belt and released my death grip from the ladder. Had I missed any German periscopes while I was adjusting my gear?

The mate on the bridge must have had the patience of a saint, for every few minutes (it seemed like an hour), I asked for the time of day. After about six calls, I decided to believe that my wristwatch was working OK.

During my long harrowing vigil, I did not spot anything. There were no periscopes, U-boats, pocket battleships, or floating debris. When I finally reached the safety of the deck, I had a headache, earache, rubber legs and a bad case of the shakes. At least the ship had been safe on my watch, and I said a silent prayer of thanks.

"Wed. May 19, 1943 Stood crow's nest watch 1200-1400. Set watch ahead for the 5th time."

Another watch in the crow's nest—aft this time. Perhaps aft watch would be better, maybe not so much wind or not so much motion. I climbed the narrow ladder with alacrity, feeling like a seasoned salt of the crow's nest watch. Had I been a seasoned salt, I would have known that aft was not the better place to be.

The sooty stack and tubes were blown at night to keep our ship's location a secret; black smoke would be a dead giveaway of our position. Although it was now daylight, the soot and carbon from last night's blow had settled on the platform and all the viewing equipment. The ear phones left smudges on my hair and eyes, and the gassy carbon choked my throat. With watery eyes and blurred vision, it was difficult to pan the horizon for anything that moved. The feeling of panic stayed with me through the watch as I wiped my eyes to clear my vision. Aft was definitely not the better watch. What a day.

"Thu. May 20, 1943 Paid today $96.00."

Paid $96.00 a month, room and board, and see the world through a porthole. Where have I heard that before? Sometimes I only took a small draft, for I did not want to carry cash while I was working. After liberty at Fort Pierce with Annie, I was flat broke, and when we arrive in Oran, Africa, it was possible that we might have a liberty. Oran sounded exciting; perhaps we would find some souvenirs to send home.

We all breathed a sigh of relief when the British surveillance aircraft joined our convoy; we knew we had to be getting close to land, but where? We would soon find out.

"Fri. May 21. 1943—12th day out."

Today the slow-moving cargo ships and merchant vessels broke away from the convoy. They had made a safe Atlantic crossing and were now headed for their particular ports of call.

"Sat. May 22, 1943 Finally sighted land today, went through the Straits of Gibralter 10:00-2:00. Passed the rock at noon and hit the Mediterranean."

We were all on deck when the bridge sighted land. I expected someone to call out "land ho" as we noticed a distant peak on the horizon. We entered the Straits of Gibraltar with a sigh of relief, for we were now in safer waters. The British escort planes dipped their wings good-bye and returned to their refueling base.

Our ship, free of the slow-moving cargo ships, picked up speed to about 12 knots. Hundreds of dolphins matched our speed and we gathered on deck to watch their playful antics across our bow. They seemed to be greeting us, and I hoped it was a good omen for the future.

Gibraltar seemed to rise straight up as we reached the central portion. My head felt a little woozy as we tried to look to the top. There was rock as far as the eye could see. We passed the center about noon, and by four o'clock we entered the beautiful waters of the Mediterranean. There was an instant change in the atmosphere; the cool, brisk winds of the Atlantic, gave way to the soft balmy caress of a tropical breeze. The curious crew covered the ship's rail, as we leaned over to view the water. It was so clean and clear we could see the bottom.

"Sun. May 23, 1943—14th day, came into harbor at Oran 10:30 A.M. Set watch for the 6th time."

The mountains of Oran appeared almost like magic, accompanied by a smell so strong we knew only waste, rot and mold could emit. This pungent smell would be our introduction to the harbor of Oran for many trips to come. I had read about the ancient city of Oran, founded in the 10th century. The Casbah, in the old quarter, was no doubt the most famous, but the centuries-old Mosque was noted for its interesting architecture. I was anxious to go ashore and see these sights that I had only read about.

Six months ago, the *Stanton* and other transports landed in Oran, and started the campaign to rid Africa of the German occupation troops. The French in Oran at this time were hostile and defended their city. Our landing boats had not been designed with ramps or with enough power for the necessary speed, and casualties were high. The French resistance finally ceased, and these invasions proved the need for a new and improved landing craft, and the intensive seamanship training to handle them. Nothing had changed in the harbor. French ships, half submerged, were used for ship anchorage. We tied up at the dock, and our soldiers were able to debark without our help. The Fort of Oran, high on the mountain, overlooked the harbor, the rocky shoreline and all ships at anchor.

Our newly designed landing craft were made by Owens, Chris Craft, and Higgins boat companies, and they were working around the clock to fill the crush of orders. This unusual design was originated by the Higgins Industries in Louisiana. Their first model was perfected to work in shallow marshes of the bayou, and operated in only 18 inches of water. The construction enabled it to run through debris without fouling the propeller, which was protected by a semi-tunnel. The sides were constructed of oak or other hard wood, with light armor plating on the sides. A metal ramp at the bow had a winch with a brake. The winch lowered the ramp quickly, enabling the troops to debark immediately upon arriving. The power from the 225 HP diesel engines, at full speed, could almost lift the boat out of the water. Mounted on the stern were two thirty-caliber machine guns for when protection was needed. Speed was of the essence, and each craft could move about 30 or more troops carrying full gear and armament, from ship to shore, in just a few minutes.

While in port, the landing craft, which were rested over the forward and aft hatches, were lowered into the water for use as the ship's ferry service, including the mail run. The other craft remained secured on deck. While in port, we were also relieved of our battle stations, but not free from watch duty. In port we had another concern; the Germans, driven out of the city, were battling our troops in the mountainous areas. Biserte was not far away, and the Germans still occupied the airport. The deck watches we were assigned to were stepped up to 4-hour shifts, and we paced all decks with 45 automatics at the ready, with orders to shoot at anything or anyone floating in the water. There were many British ships in the harbor as well as American, and German swimmers had been caught trying to place bombs on the sides of the ships and plant mines in the harbor. Our eyes and nerves were on a constant alert.

"May 25, 1943 Went on liberty in Oran, North Africa."

A liberty at last. After changing our American dollars into francs, we hopped an old trolley for the shops downtown. The trolley had an open air trailer on the back and the frustrated conductor had difficulty collecting the fares because sailors were packed everywhere, some were even hanging over the side. When we came to our stop we jumped off. He shook his fist, and yelled something in French at us. We pretended we didn't understand, which we didn't, exactly.

The stores—what was left of them—were in bad shape, for the Germans had taken everything of value when they pulled out of the city. In one dusty old shop, I found a book of post cards that contained pictures of the town hall, post office, the cathedral and the mosque. On the outer cover the words *Oran, Souvenir of North Africa* were printed, for the benefit of the tourist. I guess you could call us tourists, at this time!

We hunted for a place to get something to eat, but the Germans had taken the food also. Some of the shopkeepers beckoned us to come in; a few had tomatoes and eggs, and we were glad to get anything fresh. Tomatoes grew very well there, and a few lucky ones had hidden their chickens from the Germans.

The buildings around town were old, old, old, but the architecture was beautiful, and looked Turkish in origin. Finding little to do, we noticed an old building with the word *cinema* on the front. We took a chance and sure enough, it was a movie house. We lucked out; the movie was *Holiday Inn*. The voices were in English, and the French words were printed below the screen. Partway through the show we heard some giggling in the back of the room. The objects of our attention were several Arab girls, without their veils, necking and kissing their young men. It seemed strange, but then we were in a strange country. We had been warned before we left the ship on liberty to stay out of posted areas and always be watchful for the small cells of German snipers who threatened the outer areas of the city. There was not much else to do so we headed back to the ship.

"Fri. May 28, 1943 Married eight months today."

"Sun. May 30, 1943 Our Memorial Day. Left Oran, moved across to Mastaganem, Algeria. Picked up troops for maneuvers."

We anchored at Mastaganem, Algeria. The amphibious training base there was new, and it looked like it had been slapped together in a great hurry. The base was used as a holding station for amphibious replacement troops.

We knew hard work was cut out for us because our task was to start training the troops all about the amphibious landing procedures, and how to get them ashore in a hurry without getting them killed in the process. This was the first maneuver with the *Stanton* for our new amphibious crew, and we made many mistakes. We rehearsed the circle and the V formation, timing each practice for speed and accuracy. Some of our crew had been at the first landing in Africa, but their casualties had been high, for the boats were slow and they were not equipped for swift debarking.

"Tues. June 1, 1943 Paid today, $22.00."

I drew $22.00 from my account; I do not think our maneuvers will last much longer, but perhaps we will have another liberty in Oran. There is a possibility we will go to Algiers, if so I will need some spending money since my personal supplies are running out. We stayed at Mers el Kebir, Algeria for five days.

"Sun. June 6, 1943 Moved back to Oran. Dock with British flat top. Formidable, also two battlewagons."

Security in the harbor was greatly increased with so many powerful ships gathered at one place. Each day more ships moved in, and I could tell we were gearing up for something big. We were curious about an old tanker moored near us; the crew was Chinese. They seemed anxious for us to come aboard, and they showed us their cabins, which were quite spacious compared to our crowded transport accommodations. It seemed that they were not as interested in us as they were in our watches. They gathered around me and examined mine, with the gold letters and the dark face. Their money did not interest me; there was no way I would sell pop's watch. Some of the boys sold theirs; I guess they could buy another at the exchange, when they had a chance. Right now I really needed mine. The tanker was quite rusty and dirty; we were glad to get back to the *Stanton*.

"Thur. June 10, 1943 Left the States one month ago today."

"Fri. June 11, 1943 Took troops aboard."

The first infantry boarded to rehearse nighttime landings. The crews were issued small, blue, hooded flashlights, our only guide allowable. There was a lot for the troops to learn, and they spent time getting in shape and reading their manuals. I had been assigned to the wave commanders' craft with Ensign Spannbauer. For some reason or other I was the radioman again.

"Sat. June 12, 1943 Left Oran with a load of troops; wife's birthday tomorrow."

Training troops to land on an unfamiliar beach in the early hours of the morning was not without its mistakes. Equipment snagged in the cargo nets, soldiers misstepped from the net to the craft and lost their balance and their gear. Some of our boats beached at the wrong angle, sending cascades of water into the ramp, flooding the engines. Practice was the key word, and that is what maneuvers are for.

"Sun. June 13, 1943 Ann's birthday; 22 years old. Pulled into Algiers, went on Liberty."

We moored our ship at Point Mali, Algeria, and discharged our troops. The docks and the shoreline were a beehive of activity; in fact, from our ship's deck the fuel drums lined up on shore resembled a giant honeycomb. Trucks were all in order, parked with the jeeps in a V formation all around the outer edge. This staging area for supplies was in its place, all at the ready to be moved to the next staging or a final destination.

I'm sure the streets of Algiers had never seen so many service personnel. Sailors lined the streets, all gawking at the sixteenth-century fortress, with its ancient Casbah. Algiers was the capital city and a major seaport, and we wanted to see the sights and perhaps find a few little interesting things to send home. The Germans took everything with them when they left the city, and did not give up easily. There were pockets of German troops in the mountain areas, and they sometimes returned to the city at night to do any damage they could. We were warned to be on the alert and watch out for snipers. There were areas restricted to servicemen and we were warned to stay away, especially the Casbah.

"THUR. JUNE 17, 1943 WENT ON SECOND LIBERTY IN ALGIERS; MUCH BETTER CITY THAN ORAN."

This city was more modern and a lot cleaner than Oran. It was the seat of the government, and government buildings predominated the area. Some homes were built along the side of the mountain, in clusters, around the extensive docking area.

There was a small garrison of British marines at dockside, and they seemed quite friendly. One Brit offered to escort us and show us the city. We appreciated the offer. He was tall and raw boned, and the noise from his high-top, hobnail shoes echoed with every step he took. You can be sure no one laughed at his short britches or the thick wool socks that reached to his knees. He was a tough, seasoned Brit marine, and we were glad he was on our side.

The steep steps from the dock led to the street. The business district was deserted, and in great disrepair. The German soldiers had done a thorough job of cleaning out the city. We did find a few things to buy, for one store had some novelty leather wallets and change purses. One change purse was blue camel skin, folded to collapse into a small square. I was happy to have something to put in my sea bag to take home.

Ragged beggars were everywhere; in the alleys, on the benches, and mostly in our way. Dirty children tugged at our trousers with their rehearsed story, "Got big sister. Joe, cheap, cheap, only a dolla'." The burley Brit shoved them aside with his boot, and tossed them a few coins. He told us to just keep walking. It was hard to see the children in so much poverty, particularly the crippled ones, and many with twisted arms and bad teeth. The Arabs sleeping on benches and in the alleyways did not seem to have anything to do or anything they wanted to do. Some sleeping right in our pathway would not even move a little. We jostled one, accidentally on purpose, feeling both anger and pity. The Arab struggled to his feet in a belligerent position, all the while screaming in French. We pretended his few choice words had offended us and we took a stance, saying, "*Vous Boxaire?*" Like a puppet on a string, he disappeared into the alley, with a flash of dirty robe and feet.

The merchants were eager to sell what little they had left after the Germans (the nonpaying customers), had stripped them of everything movable. We bought a few cards and received some change in French francs for souvenirs. The paper money was written on the Banque De L'Algerie, and had pictures of nude youths kneeling and another standing with a small cloth covering his loins. The five-franc bill had a picture of a lovely lady on the front; something more to store in my sea bag.

We followed our Brit friend to the Hotel Aletti's outdoor café. All the tables were filled with servicemen and French residents. We edged our way to the end of a long table and ordered beer. I had not acquired a taste for it, but it was something to do. We were about to finish our drinks, when a lady with a small baby in her arms circulated between the tables, begging for money. I did not see her face until she got to our table. I had all I could do to keep my composure—her nose had been eaten away by some disease; was it leprosy? We donated a few coins and made a hasty exit.

The Brit was still nursing his beer with some friends, so we left the French chattering of the Aletti to explore the city on our own. The Germans had trashed the city streets, but the buildings were still in quite good shape. Our army trucks were scattered about the city parks, and it was amazing that the many statues and fountains were still in one piece. The Arab women seemed to travel in groups of five or six, shuffling about in their bulbous sheets and headscarves. They all carried large bags, some dragging on the ground and some on their shoulders. We had no idea what they were carrying.

We noticed large posters on the walls of some of the buildings, displaying a huge boot and the words, *Stamp out the Germans. Un*

Seul but Victory. We were all for that.

The narrow street seemed steeper, and soon the way became a series of stone steps. We passed an area posted off limits, but we ignored that and were soon climbing the steps to the Casbah area. I'm not sure if it was curiosity or the French beer, but we forged ahead in spite of the warnings.

The areas of apartment-type dwellings were so close to the alley, there was barely enough light to see, and the stone path was slippery with lichen and moss. We began to notice that with the musty smell there was now a strange odor of cooking. The dwellings were in tiers, and we could look right into the front doorways. We saw women sitting in the alcoves, many with young daughters in all stages of undress; women with babies sucking at their breasts, toothless hags, and graceful twelve-year-olds, all waving in our direction.

Expecting business, little ragged boys were sent to us to advertise their wares. One glance at the fleshy bosoms, and the toothless smiles was enough to send us running, but we gave the boys a few coins and headed out, fast.

We were still laughing about the beauties of the Casbah, when the MPs blocked our path. An army captain with the MPs fairly jumped out of the jeep at us. He screamed, "What in the hell do you think you are doing? Follow us down to the prophy station! Now!" We explained that we had only been in the area about a half hour, and had not even stopped walking. Anyhow, we had seen enough of the famous Casbah at Algiers.

"Sun June 27, 1943 On GQ all day."

The navy barber on deck had just finished giving me the short haircut, when out of nowhere, a German bomber slipped into the harbor and placed a direct hit on an ammunition ship. The explosion shook and bounced our ship so violently the dust from the cracks rose like a fog into the air. We rushed to the outer deck just as the chief bosun's mate piped general quarters.

This was a costly lesson; we had been caught flat-footed and napping. The Germans were still in possession of the airfield on the north end of Biserte, and it seemed the skies were suddenly filled with their zooming planes. Our anti-aircraft guns blasted away, determined to keep our ship safe at all cost.

We stayed at general quarters all day, and at dusk the attacks subsided. There was a soft cheer of relief that no more harm had been done. The explosion was a horrible lesson, and you can believe that from then on we were all on our toes.

"Mon. June 28, 1943 Married 9 mos. today."

"Thu. July 1, 1943 Got first mail since leaving the States, also a picture of Ann."

Mail at last, it had been a long two months. Ann sent a picture taken when she sang at the USO. The song kept running through my brain. It was one of our favorites, and I'm sure a favorite of all servicemen away from home. The first line was *I'll be seeing you in all the old familiar places*. How did I ever get so far away in this God forsaken country, and would she ever be seeing me again? I couldn't seem to shake that lonesome, homesick feeling from my mind.

"Sun. July 4, 1943 Had turkey dinner, and pie and ice cream, etc."

The dinner was so good we felt like prisoners on the night before the hanging. We knew something was about to happen; surely it would be an invasion. That was what we had been training for, but where?

"Mon. July 5, 1943 Paid $43.00. Loaded with troops of the 1st Inf. Div.—'The Big Red 1.'"

The decks were bulging when the First Division's 16th Regimental Combat Team boarded. Water for showers was scarce. Our tanks were filled at every port of call, but when potable water was not available we had to rely on our small desalination unit. Drinking water was the most important, and everyone learned to be very careful. Food was limited in quality with so many on board; at least the crew had their own dining room, but dining hours were also limited. There was little space on deck, but the troops made the best of it, writing letters, cleaning their equipment or resting; just glad to have a change from the training and maneuvers.

"TUES. JULY 6, 1943 LEFT THE DOCK IN ALGIERS. ANCHORED IN HARBOR WITH BRIT. *NELSON*, *RODNEY*, *HOWE*, KING GEORGE. LEFT ALGIERS FOR???"

The Brits were noted for their pomp and circumstance, and wartime was no exception. Each morning and evening, with their ships near us in the harbor, it was show time. We stood on deck and watched their color ceremony. The sound of the band playing their national anthem, as it drifted across the water, created an aura of patriotism and sadness.

King George VI arrived in Algeria to inspect and salute his troops. All the ships in the harbor were at parade dress for respect to this popular king. The H.M.S. *Howe* was near and we were on deck as we watched the transformation. All the officers and crew were on deck, lined up in perfect precision; their ship's big guns pointed skyward in salute.

The king paid his respects, and boarded the U.S.S. *Savannah* for an inspection. I was proud to observe that our troops were also a stirring sight in their parade dress.

We soon learned that the anchorage of ships in the harbor were to be a part of convoy TF81. There were hundreds of ships, battle wagons, tankers, transports, ammo craft, supply ships, aircrafts and carriers, LSTs and destroyers, to name a few. There was no doubt that an invasion was going to happen, and soon.

"WED. JULY 7, 1943 FOUND OUT TODAY WE ARE TO INVADE SICILY."

Our amphibious crew and troops were called to the aft hatch. A ping-pong table had been set up, with a papier-mâché model of our objective. The model had been created from aerial photos and pictures taken from submarine periscopes. All the beach landing areas were indicated with roads, trees, and any landmarks to give us our direction. They announced that the code name for the Gela landing would be Husky, and the code color was blue.

They passed out booklets, "Soldiers' Guide to Sicily." My main interest was the beach, and the adjoining areas; so glad I was not going with the soldiers inland. The beach area was far enough. Even the beach was much more than I had bargained for when I joined the Navy. However, I was proud of my special training, and the important part we had in moving the troops and supplies to the beaching areas. There was absolutely no doubt that we were gearing up for something really big.

"THU. JULY 8, 1943 ONE SUBMARINE SUNK AND ANOTHER SUNK ABOUT 9 P.M. AN LCI HIT A MINE."

Our anti-aircraft and destroyers were busy guarding the secrecy of our convoy as we steamed toward Sicily. We were at our battle stations on constant watch. A pack of U-boats was shadowing our convoy, and the steady boom and splash of our destroyer's depth charges kept us on edge. After the second submarine was blown up and sunk, we were sure one of our transports would be hit next, they were so close. Soon after the second sub was sunk, the pack left, and we had just settled down when a huge explosion blew an LCI all to pieces. It had hit a mine that the minesweepers had missed. One fact was true. Someone was trying to kill us. All these explosions added to my state of anxiety. I had four copies of Secret Bigots from Army HQ to memorize; all dated June 27, 1943. The cover letter of the Bigots gave directions of defense to the 1st Infantry Division and the support field force. I scanned the letter carefully to understand their objective and the amphibious cooperation needed. My #48 copy of the first Secret Bigot was a three-page summary from our intelligence service concerning the enemy situation, with new identification, and strength of movements.

There were lists of measures, handling prisoners and captured documents. It is unbelievable how much was involved, just for the handling of prisoners. They were to be immediately separated into three groups: officers, non-commissioned officers and enlisted men. After they were separated, they were to be dispatched into designated wire enclosures, and turned over to prisoner of war interrogators. A lot of paperwork was involved, including time, place, and any documents they possessed. The prisoners were to be given no food, water or cigarettes. There was to be no talking allowed, and they were to be stripped of their own iron rations and water. Any documents found were to be wrapped in their hat and coat, and forwarded to CT-S2. ID tags were not to be removed, and the prisoners could also keep their helmets, gas masks, insignia, decorations, money and personal items. I tried to memorize the maps and photographs of the field artillery battery units, for the amphibious crew had worked with the 1st Infantry, and it was our duty to provide them with a safe beach landing, if possible.

The second Secret Bigot was a summary of the enemy situation; the overall strength of their ground forces. Just to scan the list of enemy troop and field divisions left my heart pounding to say the least. The total Italian garrison was estimated at 208,500. Their four field divisions totaled 61,300, troop artillery 15,400, AA artillery 11,200, French tanks 900, Italian Lt. Tanks 350, just to name a few. I was greatly concerned with the five coastal divisions totaling 31,700. In my mind, it was unbelievable that we would soon be encountering this massive force.

The list continued with how many men were in each division, how many mortars, anti-tank guns, vehicles, artillery pieces, and tank battalions. Adding to the garrison, the Germans moved up six coastal divisions and 1,245 planes, only 700 in service.

It was a must to memorize the third Secret Bigot. If not I was dead in the sand. The photographic report, and the map reference: a possible MG position in the sand, short trench leading to MG post, trenches on top of sand dunes, bolt of wire on MG position in the dune, three gun AA battery and probable search light, two small huts, and camouflaged pillbox on the beach.

The fourth Secret Bigot contained maps with landing directions for each division. Now we were getting to the real nitty-gritty. We would debark the 1st Infantry on beaches number 67 and 68, under cover of darkness, at H-hour, on D-day. The 1st Infantry were to charge the island and capture the city of Gela and Pointe Olivio airport. There was a big F note at the bottom of the page. The Navy would provide escort, clear offshore underwater minefields to protect the transports and be prepared to assist landings with gunfire on call.

The amphibious crew now had another concern, if the Navy missed clearing a mine, at the speed of our crafts, if we made contact, four sailors and 38 infantrymen would be fish food. It was a little (very little) comforting to note that all mine fields would be guarded and marked, at least on shore.

We had another directive to remember. All watches would be synchronized with the ship's time; radio silence, until enemy contact. H-hour, D-day would be announced. Assault troops would be armed with razor-sharp bayonets. For ID in the dark, all EMs would have a white strip on their helmets. Officers would wear 3-inch bands on both arms and a vertical strip 1-inch wide and 2 inches long on back of helmet.

That night I tossed and turned, I could not sleep. The information on the Secret Bigot kept fading in and out of my mind. Would my brain be dysfunctional like in English class back home?

"Fri. July 9, 1943 Issued 45s today; tonight is 'the' night."

Sicily was near. Our amphibious crews were issued 45's and K-bar knives, sharp as razors. This was for real, no more playing the games of war. By evening, clouds moved in and the sea became choppy and dark. Soon the wind was howling through the decks, and the convoy was hit by a severe storm. The destroyers on patrol were wallowing around and crashing into the waves, visible one instant and then falling completely out of sight. The troops were bouncing around on deck, seasick and heaving over the side; again I was thankful for my strong stomach. The storm worsened as the night wore on and we became even more nervous. Would the landings have to be cancelled? There was no way we could launch our craft in such high seas in pelting rain. We had reached our rendezvous area where all the convoys had gathered, and there were ships as far as the eye could see. The sight was about as close to peril on the sea as I would like to observe. Ships of all kinds, armed and waiting, were churning, crashing and dipping. It was a small miracle that great damage was not done.

"Sat. July 10, 1943—1 A.M."

Just when we thought all was hopeless and all was lost, the storm winds eased a bit. By 1 A.M. we were assigned our anchorage area and Operation Husky was about to begin. We were issued our final orders, and given our radio call signs.

TBY Channel 37	Red Beach	
	List 1	List 2
STANTON	601	2S9
CHASE	2ER	4M1
FUNSTON	3Q1	4D1
ANDROMEDA	2E3	6A8
PROCYON	8E1	4P3
PC 591	P591	P591
BARNETT	4H9	102
DICKMAN	7C1	907
LYON	1Y4	6F8
OBERON	201	5Z9
DERWENTDALE	608	1K7
PC 624	P624	P624
PC 625	P625	P625
PC 542	P542	P542
BEACHMASTER, RED	BMR	BMR

BEACHMASTER RED 69	BMR 69	BMR 69
SALVAGE VESSEL P 69	SVR 69	SVR 69 (LCM2) HOBBS
1ST WAVE COMMANDER P69	1WR69	1WR69-69-11-STEIN-SPANNBAUER
BOAT GROUP COM P69	BGR69	BGR69(69-1) BLOOM-GARRISON
CONTROL VESSEL(PRIMARY)	CVR69	CVR69
CONT.VES. (SECONDARY)	2CVR69	2CVR69(P69-19) BARRETT-STEWART
CONT.VES.(TERTIARY)	3CVR69	3CVR69(P69-20) STORY-SPALDING

NOTE: LIST 1 EFFECTIVE UPON RECEIPT
LIST 2 EFFECTIVE UPON ORDER

"Sat. July 10, 1943 Hit beachhead at 3:15 A.M. Had a bad time of it, but got off OK. Took third load in and got beached. Stayed 7 hours on beach dodging planes. What a day."

I was on the flying bridge covering radio communications when we maneuvered the ship to our anchorage position. Our objective was the city of Gela, where the bulk of the Italian coastal division was entrenched with the German search radar crew. Gela was the central landing objective of Operation Husky, with amphibious landings at Licata to the north, and Scoglitti to our right.

Captain Dierdorff was on the bridge, issuing orders in a calm, confident manner. Observing his calm manner went a long way toward soothing my jangled nerves.

At almost 3 A.M., the first wave went ashore, loaded with their troops and ammunition. It was black dark, and we knew the beach was there, but we could not see a thing. I was concerned that the noise of our engines would alert the enemy, but with the crashing of the waves and the pelting rain, I was quite sure the enemy felt that no one would attack in such foul weather. The first wave reached the beach safely, with little resistance from the shore batteries. We had not awakened the sleeping giant, yet.

Everything changed in the blink of an eye. While we were groping our way to the shore, we were staggered with light blindness as a beam from a giant searchlight surrounded our transport and the landing area. The Germans in the city of Gela had spotted our convoy on radar, and I thought we are all dead men.

I looked up and watched as great shells passed over our heads in a slow-motioned arc. The cruiser *Savannah*, which was anchored about 8 miles out, had seen the search light, and by the time our troops were down the cargo nets, her forward turret guns were sending artillery shells blasting over our heads and into the city, putting out the lights. With the lights out, we again had to feel our way and follow the other crafts to shore. The Navy put out smoke pots to provide a landing screen for our invasion, but the garrisons had come to life and the machine gun placements were hammering us from all directions. German Messerschmitts strafed our boats, and we watched with horror as a Stuka dive-bomber struck the destroyer *Maddox* with a hit that exploded the magazine compartment with a flash of fire. The ship turned over and sank in an incredibly short time. I could not believe the nightmare scene of smoke and fire, right before our eyes. Some of the *Maddox* crew had just been aboard the *Lizzy* to watch our movies. These eager young men had only just begun to fight. War really is hell.

The first wave battled the surf and had little resistance from the shore batteries, until they hit the beach. By now there was so much booming gunfire and screams of anguish that we had difficulty communicating. Supplies and troops were piling up on the shore, and the beach master had to wave some boats aside. Jack, a coxswain on the first wave, was stranded on the beach. His boat had taken a hit and he looked like a mad man, screaming for help for his crew. One had taken a strip of machine bullets across his chest, fairly cutting him in half. His other crewman had taken a shell across the side of his face ripping his eye from the socket. Blood was gushing everywhere. Jack dragged them to a sand dune, out of the line of fire, to put them on the next boat. The lieutenant on the next boat, in a barrage of fire, refused to go ashore and returned his boatload back to the ship. By the time the next craft arrived and was unloaded, one of Jack's crew was dead, and the other had lost so much blood, he had stopped screaming.

(Later, Jack was awarded the Silver Star for bravery. The doctor of surgery, from the Boston area, said the crewman could have been saved, if he had arrived just a few minutes earlier. Jack's other crewman had a nervous collapse, and was sent to the hospital in Algiers. The lieutenant who turned back was court-martialed for dereliction of duty; we all knew how he felt, we were all afraid, but we had a job to do and we did it.)

By this time, we could barely get to the shore; the German Messerschmitts were strafing the beach like hornets. Dawn arrived; they spotted our transports and opened up with everything they had in defense of their island. There was no turning back, and we crouched down in the boat with the troops, trying to avoid the sniper and machine gun fire. We were being peppered unmercifully, and the officer ordered, "Crawl out, crawl out fast!" I would have to wait until next trip to dig my foxhole in the sand, for the troops were bunching up at the exit, while I was trying to balance my radio and close the ramp at the same time. Jonesie the coxswain was crouched below the bulkhead, trying to avoid the machine gun fire and back off the beach at the same time. I was caught at the closing ramp by an exiting soldier. He crashed into me, swiping my head with his bayonet. Blood was spurting over my earphones as I made a giant leap over the rising ramp. The coxswain kept screaming, "Shut that ramp, shut that ramp," as if I wasn't doing my damndest to do just that. I should have been given a medal for my fancy footwork, as I tried to avoid crushing the wounded infantrymen left in the boat. One wounded man was screaming "My bella, my bella." I could not understand what he was saying, but I located a wound in his stomach; I was not accustomed to the Carolina accents. When I unfastened his web belt, blood gushed out and a bullet fell to the deck; it had gone completely through his stomach.

I had never administrated a shot of any kind before, but I got the morphine needle from the kit and jabbed away, then I applied a good dose of sulfa. Blood was dripping from my forehead; I didn't know that my cut was so deep.

Meanwhile, the army corporal, who had been shot in the calf of his leg, was hopping around on one foot, cussing up a storm. We opened up the engine and fairly flew back to the ship. The crew lowered a stretcher and hauled the wounded to the deck where they were given emergency care by the corpsmen. The grateful private gave me his carbine, and I found a hiding place for it near my bunk.

Just when I thought things couldn't get any worse, on the trip back to the shore the surf changed and the waves dashed our boats about. Several were already beached, still loaded. Giant waves washed up the ramp and flooded our engine with seawater. We all pitched in to help each other unload before the water ruined the ammo. I watched for my chance, and between bursts of machine gun fire, I dug my foxhole. Supplies were piling up on shore, for the army had so much resistance from the enemy, they could not get a chance to move anything. We had almost finished unloading, when a German ME109 Messerschmitt strafed the beach and headed for our boat. Thank God I had dug that foxhole! A string of machine gun fire peppered the sand at my heels as I tried to run in the damp sand. My feet felt like lead as the sand kept pulling me back, but I made a giant leap to safety. With a sudden jolt, I felt a stunning blow at the back of my head. Blood splashed in my eyes and I thought my time had come. When my head and eyes cleared a bit, a soldier's boot was in my face and I had a mouth full of sand.

To say I was mad as hell, was putting it mildly. The soldier had jumped into my foxhole and the butt of his gun had cracked my head. The cut over my eye was gushing blood, and I thought if I got any more cuts I'd need a transfusion. I had arrived as a rookie on my first invasion, but now I was a combat veteran in just four hours.

Supplies were still piling up and we would move a pile and then jump in our foxhole. I kept remembering my grandfather saying, "The scareder you are, the harder you work," and by now we were really working hard. There just was not any let up. I kept wondering where our air support was and why someone didn't clear out those machine gun nests. The Germans had given us seven hours of pure hell.

Finally, the Navy sent in heavy salvage boats to tow the disabled craft from the beach. Some were on their sides in the water, damaged beyond repair, and we had no transportation back to the ship. We spent so much time running to our foxholes, we couldn't even assess our damage. I thought the day of hell would never end. It was getting dark, and the tide was lapping at the supplies on the beach. I hoped the enemy was as worn out as we were. The lieutenant helped us attach a towline to one of the boats to tow it back to the ship where we could work on it. LST #313, loaded with heavy equipment, had been beached. With a droning roar, a Stuka dive-bomber made a direct hit. The concussion blew the men up in the air and out into the water. We were able to make a quick turn, lower our ramp to the water level, and scoop them up. We now had a full load in our boat and a disabled boat in tow. Our speed was so slow, I was afraid we would be an easy target, but we finally made it back to the ship.

I hurried to my bunk, not to sleep, but to check on the prized carbine. Gone! While I was dodging bullets on the beach, someone from ship's company had found it. I was bone tired and muscle sore, but there was no time for sleep. I had a watch to stand, but who could sleep anyway after today? This day had been my worst nightmare, and my legs were still shaking. The ship's superstructure was now my safe haven, and I huddled in the dark, worried about what I would do right now if the ship was hit. I really had no idea. Our amphibious group was not a regular part of ship's company, and we were on deck with our boats most of the time. We had a survival plan; if the ship was hit we would swing out on the large knotted ropes used to lower our crafts, and drop free of the ship. The one flaw in our plan: a direct hit.

Later I checked the infirmary because I was concerned about the Carolina boy's stomach wound. The doc said we had probably saved his life with our quick reaction and speedy return because he had been bleeding internally. This news was like a shot in the arm, and I returned to work with renewed energy and determination. At least something had gone right today.

"SUN. JULY 11, 1943 HIT BEACH LITTLE AFTER NOON WITH AMMO, AND FLOODED. SPENT 5 VERY ACTIVE HOURS ON THE BEACH. AT 10 P.M. PLANES CAME OVER AND BOMBED FOR 1 HOUR. TERRIBLE NIGHT."

We had been practicing for war, but now the real thing was upon us. Our first day had been hell and the 1st Infantry needed more support from somewhere. They fought like tigers to push their way to Gela, but the opposition and the attacks from the air were overwhelming. The German airpower was in control of the beach and our landing craft were being riddled with bullets. We were worried that the army would be pushed back into our faces.

The cruisers finally received some communication and they sent floatplanes out looking for targets, and at dawn they started their own bombardments. The cruisers *Savannah* and *Boise*, back in action after repairs, along with other destroyers, pounded the shore batteries and destroyed about one half of the German tanks. The Italian troops had enough, and fled for their lives, leaving guns, ammo, and personal belongings behind. We were up early, for our boats had taken a beating yesterday. There was not much we could do about the machine gun holes, but we patched the damage and checked the engines for wear and tear.

The bombardment was still underway after noon, when we loaded the boats with ammo, and hit the beach. There was no time to think, but I knew we had to break the record for unloading that ammo between strafings, or our bodies would be splattered all over the island of Sicily.

By mid-afternoon we thought the bombers were quieting down. We were half way to shore when we saw paratroopers above us. At first, all we could think of was that the Germans were attacking from the sky. Then we discovered that our own anti-aircraft guns had hit the transport airplanes towing our gliders. Apparently communications had been fouled up, for we could see it was our own men. The next few moments were so frantic and unbelievable that I can't remember how many paratroopers we fished out of the water, but we knew the

Stukas would have a turkey shoot if they came back and saw them so helpless.

When we lost time with extra things, we had to rush all the more to finish unloading by the end of the day. Our next trip to shore was more bad luck. Just when we thought we had the riptide conquered, a giant wave slapped the side of our boat and the flume of water up our ramp fairly washed us away. The boat broached on its side, and the engine went dead. We had no place to go but the beach. I was bone weary from yesterday and I knew the beach was not a good place to be. Between strafings, we tried to make the wounded men more comfortable. At any time the Messerschmitts could strafe the beach, and now our boat was disabled. We waited quite a while for more transportation, and finally we were able to get them back to the ship's infirmary for emergency care.

About 10 P.M., the enemy aircraft located our transports, and German planes headed for the kill. They swooped down and dropped parachute flares that lit up our anchorage like daylight. The flares were followed by bombs, which missed our ship and exploded between the transports, blowing giant fountains of water into the air. The bosuns' mate nervously paced up and down the deck, not making my nerves any calmer. I stayed in the protection of the bulkhead, trying to ease my quivering stomach. A Stuka came in low and dove at a British ship; their big guns let loose with a blast of razor sharp scrap metal, and pieces were flying everywhere. The deck was getting peppered, and I remembered shouting to the crew, "For God's sake, keep your heads down; unless you want your face shredded." Our anti-aircraft guns were firing with a vengeance, and the booming and rocking continued for over an hour. It seemed like a lifetime.

That night I could not sleep. How many cans of fuel, ammo and blue cans of water had passed through our hands that day? Would I ever stop shaking? I was still alive, but many from the *Maddox* and the landing invasion were not. I dozed on and off all night, leaning against my landing craft in full gear, ready for the next day.

"MON. JULY 12, 1943 PULLED OUT 5 P.M. WHAT A RELIEF TO GET AWAY FROM THERE."

Our casualties replaced the infantry and cargo, and the decks were covered with stretchers and the walking wounded. We had plenty of repairs to make on our landing crafts, for machine gun damage had left strips of holes above and near the water line, and some of our boats were so damaged they had to be left behind on the shore. We checked the damage and walked up what was left of the beach; it was now free of gunfire but still dangerous with possible land mines or unexploded bombs.

I was anxious to see where the machine gun fire had been coming from. It was no wonder they could not be seen from any angle. The thick cement underground bunkers, with only a narrow gun slot visible, were covered with sand and several months' growth of weeds. There were wooden plank steps at the back, which led to a series of underground rooms. Platforms for the machine guns were built inside, with just the tip of the gun poking through the slot, visible from the outside. I guess their dawn really did come up like thunder when they saw our massive invasion force move like a tidal wave toward their garrison.

We moved through the bunkers with caution; however, from all indications, they had been in a tremendous hurry to retreat. Personal belongings were left behind seemingly with no attempt to collect anything but their clothes. The troops had been living in this bunker for quite a while. Letters, shaving equipment, combs and brushes were arranged neatly, and we were surprised that they left so much behind. An Italian helmet, with the name AVELINI printed inside, lay on the floor just inside the door. I can't imagine being in such a hurry as to leave your helmet behind. They also left ammunition behind, some boxes were full and some half empty, and some empty boxes served as little tables for their belongings. In the second area I noticed a German wrist compass on a bunk. Perhaps he had no time to strap it to his wrist. I checked the printing on the back, and it was marked BELMARK-KADIEC. Their equipment was far superior to the Italian and even more so than our own. The German mess kits utensils were heavy stainless steel, and their unique can opener had a slot on the back of the handle where their knife, fork and spoon slid together in a neat little package; this I had to save.

Near the exit, I saw what I thought was a German bayonet, partially buried in the sand. I took another precious second to wipe it off and slip it in my belt.

I pushed as many things as I could in my shirt … a small reward for the beating we had taken from the enemy. We had no more time to waste, for we still had wounded arriving to transport to the ship, and from there, transport to the hospital in Algiers. We also had taken on a few Italian prisoners and they were happy and smiling. Soon they were singing and we couldn't help feeling happy for them. They were going to America. (Where I would like to be going.) The ship was to pull anchor at 5 P.M., and we were all happy to leave Sicily behind in the care of the Army.

The *Stanton* left many landing craft behind. Although some had been riddled with bullets, flooded or crashed due to the unusually rough surf, and considering the fierce enemy resistance, the Sicilian invasion was the proving ground for the efficient work of amphibious craft and their advanced planning.

Author's Note: In my copy of the September 1943 *Our Navy* magazine, Rear Admiral Alan Kirk, head of all of the Atlantic Amphibious Training, gave a glowing account of the U.S. sailors who worked day and night for over 72 hours without rest or food. Some boats were in bad shape, but unloading was accomplished in record time.

"THU. JULY 15, 1943 PULLED INTO ALGIERS 7 A.M. TO UNLOAD OUR CASUALTIES."

The busy harbor at Algiers was host to various British and American ships. The unloading of casualties was slow and laborious. Many on the stretchers were a dead weight, and some had various braces or bulky dressings. Our debarking was treacherous to say the least. If a weight shifted we had to take special care. They were all suffering enough without being dumped into the oily harbor water.

They would soon have hospital care, and some of the more serious would be sent back to the States.

"FRI. JULY 16, 1943 GOT THREE VERY WELCOME LETTERS, ALL V-MAIL, ONE FROM ANN, HOME, AND MY FRIEND DAVE."

V-mail was a quicker, cheaper way of sending mail during the war to the troops overseas. It was small and only one page. The person sending one would go to the post office and fill out a special form that only had a few lines. The post office would photograph it and send it along with other ones going to the same general area where they were enlarged, divided up by ship and sent on. Since it was so short, V-mail was not as good as an airmail letter, but having been without mail for so long, they were a welcome sight. Our carefree days seemed so long ago, and definitely far away.

After mail call we were ordered into parade dress uniform for the funeral service of a shipmate killed at Sicily. The cemetery at Algiers was dusty, hot, and barren, and there were many new graves; a stark reminder that the battle for Sicily had taken its toll. There was no grass; there were no flowers, just a box covered with our red white and blue American flag. Someone had outlined each gravesite with white limestone rocks the size of a tiny football. A temporary marker was at each place and the cemetery resembled a huge rock garden.

Back at the ship, the bosun piped an announcement for an assembly on the main deck. Many had been wounded at the invasion of Gela, and the captain presented the Purple Heart commendations. There were several other awards and the ship's ribbon display received a second battle star; the first for Africa, and now one for Sicily.

The captain made an announcement to the assembly. "The following entry is now being made in each man's service record: 'July 9-12, 1943, participated honorably in amphibious landing, 16th combat team, U.S. Army, on beaches near Gela, Sicily, in face of strong air and land opposition.' Our ship also received a dispatch from W.A. Wiedman, Commander USNR Executive Officer, commending the speed and success of the attack and the cooperation of each member and team."

"TUES. JULY 20, 1943 PAID $21 TODAY, SENT $100 HOME."

"THU. JULY 22, 1943 LEFT HOME SIX MONTHS AGO TODAY."

"FRI. JULY 23, 1943 LEFT ALGIERS FOR ORAN."

"SAT. JULY 24, 1943 PULLED INTO ORAN THIS MORNING, ANCHORED AT MERS EL KEBIR."

In November 1942, the British had encountered the French fleet at Mers, and a French battleship, which had been sunk in the harbor, gave us a secure place to attach our lines. As we were attempting to tie up, a sudden tropical storm hit us broadside, and whipped the ship around, banging it into the other ships and the dock. The crashing jolt alerted everyone, still nervous from the last invasion, and the officer of the deck was shouting orders to reverse and secure the lines. Even the captain appeared in his striped pajamas. I'm sure he had been sound asleep after the grueling days of the invasion, and probably thought the ship was again under enemy attack. After the storm, the *Lizzy* had another battle scar, a big steel patch welded over the hole made at Mers el Kebir.

"MON. JULY 26, 1943 GOT 10 LETTERS TODAY, FIVE FROM ANN, THREE FROM THE FOLKS AND TWO FROM AUNT MABEL."

"TUES. JULY 27, 1943 WENT TO THE AMERICAN RED CROSS EMPIRE CLUB."

The Red Cross Club was a little touch of home, and the whole ship invaded its halls. When you entered, they issued you a chit for recording purposes, and my first chit was numbered 3811. I wondered if I was the 3811th serviceman to enter or what? The lobby was quite large, and they had a shelf with large black books chained to the counter. There was a section labeled for each state, and the books already had a lot of names in the New Jersey section. I could not believe my eyes. Right at the top of the list was the name, Corporal William S. Allen. Bill must have been in Oran for quite a while. I knew he was in anti-aircraft, and I hoped they had not moved on. I signed the register, and drew a large arrow from my name to his and wrote in the name of my ship and the date. Was it possible that I would be seeing my best buddy so far away from home? I was light hearted with anticipation as I jumped on the big 10x10 truck that took us on the winding road around the mountain from Oran to Mers el Kebir where the ship was tied up. We appreciated the big army trucks, for we often passed the local transportation. The buses were so slow in higher elevations, it was faster to walk. The engine was fueled by a big square stove on the back of the bus. How the apparatus ran the engine I don't know, but they had to stop and put wood or coal in the stove every so often.

"Wed. July 28, 1943 Married 10 mos. today, mailed $100 to Ann today."

"Fri. July 30, 1943 Got seven letters today."

"Fri. Aug. 5, 1943 Paid today $25."

It felt great to go ashore and stretch our sea legs. The army had a big mess tent, with wood on the sides, where we could get a little different food other than beans and corn bread, and the army trucks were always available at the dock to take us up the dusty, winding road to Oran, where we could buy a few drinks. The first place I checked was the register at the Red Cross Club. I was deflated; there was no note from Bill in the big book. A French ship was in port, and their sailors seemed friendly, especially when they heard my limited

French. (About four words.) Their offer to show us the town was accepted for we needed all the language assistance we could get. We heard, via the grapevine, that a few bars of soap and a few cigars could get us some super service, so we were prepared with a little gratuity in our pockets.

We stopped at a bar that later became my favorite, and I returned many times. It was very dark when we entered, and I felt like a bit player in an old Bogart movie. The slow-moving ceiling fan clicked away, spreading a fermented scent of stale beer and stale cooking to every corner of the room.

The chef (bartender, proprietor) greeted me with a handshake and a booming; "*Bon jour, bon jour.*" He fit into the picture, just as I had imagined. He was short with a plump girth, and a big, black handle-bar mustache. The black satin vest, covering his ample chest, had seen better days, but even with the spots it gave him a formal, proprietary air. My mental picture was complete, when his lovely, plump wife kept bobbing in and out from the back room. Yes, like in the movie, the doorway had hanging beads that jangled softly in the breeze from the fan.

When I laid the soap and the cigars on the bar, I felt as though I had performed a magic act, for Chef grinned from ear to ear while pumping my arm up and down, almost jerking my arm from its socket. "*Merci beaucoup*," he kept repeating over and over, with more bowing and shoulder pounding.

Hearing the commotion, his wife burst from the back with a squeal, and performing a magic trick of her own, she scooped up the soap in a flash, and it disappeared in the folds of her ample bosom.

Chef insisted I have a glass of homemade wine, on the house. It tasted better than I thought it would, and I was soon on my third, just sitting at the bar watching Chef pull the big, brass handle up and down, up and down. Just when I thought the fan was spinning out of whack, I realized it was my head, and my stomach was rebelling. Stein, with the cast iron stomach, was going to be sick. Voices were fading and I barely heard Chef ordering the boys to get me on the army truck.

The truck was too high. The boys tried to hoist me aboard, but my legs would not go in the same direction. Then they gave me a lift and a huge shove from the rear, and I landed on the end seat. In spite of further discouragement, I lost every thing I had eaten all day. The next morning I was sick as a dog, and had to endure the embarrassing tales of my drag up the gangway. My face looked green for a week, and I vowed there would be no more homemade wine for me … period.

My bunk was now down with the ship's company, for the cooks needed my help, and I really enjoyed it. When I was not on amphibious duty, I was up at 5 A.M., frying eggs (when we had them) or beating, up powdered eggs with water for scrambling. Sometimes the powdered eggs were a green color. (I still don't like green.)

"Tues. Aug. 10, 1943 Got letter from A. Mabel and Bill Allen today."

I was getting more frustrated every day. The letter from Bill was almost three weeks old, and I had no idea from his letter where he was located. Apparently, he had not seen my message. Information was tight, but I figured he must be here in Oran, for the units were still fighting here.

We lost one of our amphibious crew to the galley, when they discovered he had been a cook in a lumber camp in Maine. I was glad to have him for my friend for he was a huge Canuck, named Gere, with the massive arms of a lumberjack. I was soon down in the galley cooking and scrubbing with him in my off time from the boats, and when at sea I reported there for duty 24 hours on and 24 hours off. Now I was out of my jeans and into whites, which I liked. The side benefits were something to write home about; like exchanging a steak with the ice cream chef for a carton of ice cream, or go to the next deck up and exchange some of the ice cream for an apple pie. I became more popular with my crewmates, who would come down and bum a sandwich or two. (No wonder I gained about 15 pounds on the trip home, but I had lost so much weight I needed all I could get.)

"WED. AUG. 11, 1943 LEFT ORAN TODAY FOR MANEUVERS WITH TROOPS."

The 36th Infantry Division boarded with all their gear and artillery. The decks were packed and moving about was difficult; worst of all, water was at a premium again. We were busy long hours of the day, with a shipload of new troops to teach the landing procedures to. The coast of Algiers became our training ground and the infantry developed a strong bond with the navy amphibs, for we were their lifelines to a successful invasion. Soon they were perfecting their speed up and down the cargo nets, and adjusting their debarking with the tides. When our work was over, they went inland to train for that part of the invasion about to come.

"THU. AUG. 12, 1943 GOT A LETTER FROM ANN AND AUNT MABEL TODAY."

"SAT. AUG. 14, 1943 MANEUVERS OVER. TONIGHT ANCHORED AT MERS EL KEBIR."

"THU. AUG. 19, 1943 MOVED FROM MERS EL KEBIR TO DOCK AT ORAN."

"SAT. AUG. 21, 1943 HAD A PLEASANT SURPRISE WHEN BILL CAME ABOARD TONIGHT. TALKED OVER OLD TIMES AND NEW ONES. MET ANN FIVE YEARS AGO THIS MONTH. THE BEST THING THAT EVER HAPPENED TO ME."

My landing craft was over the side of the ship, and I was scouring the black boot marks from the bulkhead. Army maneuvers had left my formerly spit and polished boat in a sorry state. My crew had become friendly with the "grunts," and they were worth the extra scrubbing for they had a dirty job to do after we got them to the beach. Lost in thought, I heard an old familiar voice from above yelling, "Hey, Bill!" I had almost given up hope, and there he was. Bill had found me and he was up on the top deck, calling my name.

I secured my boat, and fairly flew up the ladder to give him a giant bear hug. He had chow with us on the ship, and we talked non-stop until very late. When he finally got to town to see my note, he rushed to Mers to find the *Stanton* had left for maneuvers, and that explained the long wait to find each other.

We hashed and rehashed our camping trips, laughed about the farmer who chased us from his corn field with a shotgun, and remembered how good the stolen corn and tomatoes tasted cooked over a campfire. Of course we recalled the prom when he stepped on Jane's (Dave's sister) dress and ripped the bottom of her skirt off. Annie lent her an under slip, and it looked as pretty as the dress, but Jane was furious. We both had to laugh about the gardenia corsages that turned black, from touching and smelling too much, before the dance even started.

After he left for his base, I was sick for home, Annie, Woodbury High, and all the growing-up things we had been lucky enough to experience before the tragedy of war.

"SUN. AUG. 22, 1943 MADE LIBERTY IN ORAN WITH BILL TODAY. SURE GLAD TO BE WITH HIM AGAIN."

The buildings in the city of Oran were beautiful, in spite of the damage from the German occupation. I met Bill at the park with its elegant statues and fountains. There were rows of giant palms around the border, and the view of the harbor was like a picture post card. It had been months since I had seen a woman, and we both stared like school kids (well, we were school kids) at the flowing silk robes, and the soft sound of their voices. For Bill, the romantic, there was always a woman, some real and some imagined, and I had a great imagination myself. He discussed a recent English flame, but admitted the flame was burning low, for his company was always on the move. It did my heart and soul good just to listen to him and inhale the aroma of his pipe.

His anti-aircraft base was next to the fort of Santa Cruz,

overlooking the city, and we ate together at his mess hall. He seemed anxious for me to meet his friends at the fort, and I had a feeling he wanted to show me how his French had improved, especially since it was a lot better than my limited vocabulary.

The French soldiers stood about in various stages of dress, some polishing their gear, and some cleaning their boots and guns. Who would imagine that two kids from Wenonah, New Jersey, would be rubbing elbows with the hardened soldiers of the French Foreign Legion? Their colorful uniforms reminded me of a scene from *Gunga Din*.

Everything seemed unreal; the snow-white trousers, the khaki fatigues, and the hat. That rakish hat gave the uniform a continental flair. In the fort, the white sun flaps were neatly folded back, but on the desert, the flaps shielded them from the merciless sun.

We chatted until our limited French ran out, and then Bill wanted to take me out of town to a farmhouse where he took his laundry. The farm couple had a daughter about 12 years old, and they talked so fast, I couldn't understand what they said; I did understand the international language, food. They insisted we sit at their big table and share their supper of eggs and tomatoes. Bill had brought them a package of soap and cigars, and I was amazed at their humble gratitude. They had so little but shared what they did have with strangers.

"Mon. Aug. 23, 1943 Left home seven months ago today, end of third month in Africa."

"Tues. Aug. 24, 1943 Met my buddy Frankie at Red Cross today. Had a good liberty. Bill came aboard again tonight."

"Wed. Aug. 25, 1943 No mail yet. Has been a while since last letter."

We had a surprise announcement this morning. The bosun piped, "Attention all hands. At 1500 this evening, the French USO troupe will come aboard to present a show for your enjoyment." The boat crew had been bone tired and weary, but when the announcement was made, there was a mad rush to the shower room. The landing craft were removed from the main deck, and everything was shoved back. This made a nice stage area where all could see. Of course the captain and the officers had a front row seat, as you know, rank has its privileges. You can be sure we all clapped and whistled as they entertained with accordions, harmonicas, and their husky French voices. Some of our division stood at the rail of the lower bridge and Storey leaned over so far he almost fell through the rail and onto the stage. Had we not been muscle hard and quick, Storey would have been stoned to death for ruining the USO show.

Girls, girls, girls, we had not seen many girls, especially singing and dancing, for a long, long while. To tell the truth, they could have been old hags, but they were young, and even in their mismatched costumes, and their strange variety of footwear, they all looked like Miss America to us. I saw the captain looking at the dancers and the young legs, and he puffed pretty hard on his pipe.

"Aug. 26, 1943 One Letter from Mr. Pfeifer, none from home or Ann. Can't imagine what is wrong."

"Fri. Aug. 27, 1943 Left dock at Oran today for maneuvers."

We boarded the 36th infantry today for more maneuvers.

"Sat. Aug. 28, 1943 Married 11 mos. today. Maneuvers over this morning, back to Mers again."

"SUN. AUG. 29, 1943 LONE ENEMY PLANE OVER TODAY."

We could hear the busy anti-aircraft guns up above in the mountains; perhaps it was Bill's unit. The Germans were tenacious about retreating farther; the ship kept a tight watch, and we were all on alert for a GQ call. A lone enemy plane escaped the barrage and slipped through, causing a lot of scrambling for cover. Our guns gave him a scare, and he hightailed it around the mountain. A German air base on the nearby island of Pantelaria was still occupied by the Germans, and they were constantly tracking our transport movements. We would rest a lot easier when our destroyers were in position to render the airstrip and their planes in a useless condition. We could see a lot of flashes and hear a lot of booming in the direction of Bill's unit, and I hoped that he was safe.

"WED. SEPT. 1, 1943 ENEMY PLANES CAME WITHIN 10 MI. AT 18,000 FT., BUT COULD NOT GET OVER."

It was evident the German planes had located the anchorage of our transports, for the anti-aircraft units were now firing around the clock. It was a good feeling to know that Bill's unit was protecting us and stranger yet to realize we were both here fighting so far from home. I prayed he would be safe.

"SAT. SEPT. 4, 1943 GOT TWO LETTERS FROM ANN TODAY, ALSO PICTURES. SURE MISS HER A LOT. HAD TWO GENERAL QUARTERS TODAY, BUT PLANES DID NOT COME OVER. SAW FRANKIE AGAIN."

I noticed the *Funston* was in port with many other transports. I knew Frankie would be somewhere in town, and I saw him at the RC club. He was worried about Esther, and I could not blame him. We were both uneasy about our next amphibious landing. It was very evident that we would attack somewhere in Italy. The Italians did not seem to be too tenacious, but the Germans were another matter. Their

Panzer Division had been sent to Italy, and Kesselring was a master at building strong points of resistance. We would need a lot of luck.

"Sun. Sept. 5, 1943 Left harbor at Mers and anchored in harbor at Oran, with the 36th Div. bound for Italy."

We did not need an announcement to know Italy was our next destination, and on September 8, we entered the Bay of Salerno, Italy. Our large convoy TF81 was close to its destination. While we were underway, the colonel and the captain announced from the superstructure that the Italians had surrendered. It was good news, and we cheered and it felt real good, feeling enemy resistance was crumbling. The code name for the invasion of Salerno was to be Avalanche, but we were soon to find out that the avalanche would be struck head on by the Germans.

"Sept. 9, 1943 Invaded Salerno, Italy, this morning. Hit the beach at 6:30 under heavy shellfire."

Although the Italians had surrendered, I was extremely nervous about the German resistance. We did not have the advantage of surprise, for they were ready. All had looked peaceful, serene and deserted. The tall weeds in the field near the beach were waving peacefully in a light breeze. A large mountain hovered in the background, and in the foreground a huge stone silo stood a lonely watch over the harbor. A long dilapidated building, missing all its windows and doors, was the only other building remaining.

The shoreline was so shallow; we could not go all the way to the beach, and before we touched the sand, all hell broke loose. The old silo seemed to explode with mortar shells and machine gun fire. The air was full of missiles, and the first wave of infantry was being pelted unmercifully. The advance groups had their hands full searching for land mines. It was a slow process, but it had to be done if the infantry was going to press inland. With their bayonets softly combing the area, they crawled on their hands and knees to locate the mines and mark them with poles and white banners.

In the midst of all this concentrated action, we were trying to unload between mortar explosions and gunfire. We hated the mortars most of all; no warning, just a big *bloop*, and you were gone, gone, gone. Our ammo boxes were really too heavy for one man to lift, but we were being pelted and the going was slow, so with the strength of fear we grabbed the cases and ran with all our might. Then they got their sights on us and we were pinned down in the protection of our boat. With pounding hearts we tried to find a way to bring up those supplies. Partway up the beach, there was an old truck half submerged in the sand. With a supreme effort, we grabbed the supplies and made a mad dash for the safety of the truck barricade. With this divided target we were able to continue unloading, for the infantry needed all the help they could get. There had been no pre-invasion bombing, which would have saved many lives, and the landing crafts had no close fire support or gunboats to protect them. The enemy was not surprised, for Kesselring's Panzer Division had saturated the area with machine gun and tank placements.

By afternoon, it was steamy hot, and we had been wading in water up to our waist for many hours; the beach was too shallow for the boats to come close to shore. We peeled off our shirts, which had been soaked and dried many times. They were white as snow and stiff as a board with drying salt water. Next to go were the dungarees. No, we did not discard them. There was no way we would part with our work pants, the back pocket held our only valuable possessions; our wallets containing pictures, money and driver's license. We learned early on to secure all in a strong rubber tied in a knot, after the heartbreak of ruined pictures and soggy ID papers. We rolled our pant legs up to our groin, and ignored the burns from the sun and the drying white salt on our skin and in our hair. There was a pile of soggy shoes kicked up on the beach, but I kept mine on, my size twelve feet were sure to step on something sharp.

By nightfall the navy cruisers *Philadelphia*, *Savannah*, and others sent out floatplanes, which located and destroyed the enemy batteries and tanks; the 36th Division was eternally grateful.

The battle for Salerno was fiercely contested, and our infantry, artillery and navy guns fought back ferociously against the barrage from the German tanks. There is no doubt that the battle for Salerno ranks with the battles on the beaches of Anzio, Tarawa and Normandy.

"Fri. Sept. 10, 1943 Chased from bay by Stukas. Bombed heavily for one hour with several near misses."

There seemed to be no end to the bombing by the German Stukas, and we kept changing our positions to finish the unloading. We almost had another direct hit, and our anti-aircraft answered their attack with a fierce barrage of gunfire. American and British troops were struggling under fierce resistance on shore, and the Navy gave the entire area a massive sweep of gunfire. Our allied troops could then move inland, and this turned the tide of the battle, proving the need for pre-invasion bombing by the Navy's big guns. Unfortunately at this time, the German Luftwaffe introduced a new weapon, a guide bomb, radio directed by an airplane high above. There were about sixteen war ships in the area, and bombs hit the *Savannah* and missed the *Philadelphia* on both sides. The British ship *Uganda* was struck through all the decks, which resulted in a crippling explosion. After another close call to our ship, I kept thinking, *A miss is as good as a mile*, and I was happy when we moved out of Salerno Harbor. The next day we departed the area.

"Tues. Sept. 14, 1943 Anchored at Mers El Kebir this morning."

We had been to Mers so often it was beginning to feel like home. Bill's anti-aircraft unit had moved on to Italy where all the action was, and I knew we would soon be returning there when we were loaded up. There was no rest, for we were constantly moving supplies and men where they were needed.

"WED. SEPT. 15, 1943 SENT $125 HOME TODAY."

"FRI. SEPT. 24, 1943 STARTED THE LOADING OF SHIP TODAY WITH CARGO OF TRUCKS AND SUPPLIES."

"TUES. SEPT. 28, 1943 MARRIED ONE YEAR AGO TODAY, STARTED STRIKING FOR COOK."

The chief commissary steward was glad to see me back in the galley, and Hank, cook 1st class, seemed to like me, and he encouraged me to strike for cook. It was very tempting, and I thought of the long hours laboring on the beach without food, and only the misappropriated cans of food to sustain us. Hank was so easy to work with, and one thing was certain, there were fringe benefits.

My bubble burst when the amphibious director said, "Absolutely no!" And that was that. I had been specially trained and they needed me. This was one time it would have been nice not to be needed.

"WED. SEPT. 29, 1943 LEFT ORAN WITH TROOPS FOR ITALY. DESTINATION AS YET UNKNOWN. AIR CORP GROUND CREW ABOARD."

"SAT. OCT. 2, 1943 ENLISTED ONE YEAR AGO TODAY. WHAT A MISTAKE. PULLED INTO HARBOR OF BISERTE, AND ANCHORED. PROBABLY WAITING FOR MINES TO BE CLEARED FROM THE NAPLES HARBOR."

"TUES. OCT. 5, 1943 LEFT BISERTE THIS MORNING AT 6 A.M."

"WED. OCT. 6, 1943 PASSED THE ISLE OF CAPRI AND ANCHORED OFF ITALY IN HARBOR OFF NAPLES OPPOSITE MT. VESUVIUS AT NOON."

All we could see was a huge rock rising out of the water, certainly nothing to write a song about, but I soon found that the view from the ocean side presented a different picture. The area was more sloping, and there were buildings along the mountainside. The scenery was striking with lush green shrubbery, which almost covered the ancient ruins of the villas of Roman emperors.

The entrance to Naples Harbor gave us an excellent view of the famous Mount Vesuvius, and we stood on deck and watched as the great volcano spewed black smoke and rumbled gently.

The view at night was more impressive with the red glow and the belching flames. The *Stanton* was the first Allied ship in the harbor, and there was so much debris, we could not get near the dock. The area looked like a maritime graveyard, and we had to anchor out and lower our boats for debarkation. The Germans, as they evacuated, masterminded a total destruction of the harbor. All the storage areas at dockside were gutted and windows were blown out. Timing devices exploded and reduced the cranes and oil tanks to masses of twisted steel and scrap metal. A hospital ship had been blown apart and turned on its side, blocking the channel, along with smaller boats and barges. More bad luck for our boats, there was a thick coat of heavy black oil in the water, and it stuck to everything. As if that was not enough, there was a high sea wall for the troops to cross. Behind the sea wall there was a huge ancient castle. It had a large turret, and all around the top there were stone notches where the ancient protectors of the castle rested their guns. I was surprised that there were no German defenders in view. The troops had a bit of difficulty crossing the high seawall, but at least there was no resistance, for the enemy had evacuated. The troops debarked safely with little more than thick, black oil on their boots. What a relief.

"THU. OCT. 7, 1943 FINISHED DISCHARGING

CARGO, AND LEFT NAPLES ABOUT 2:00 P.M., IN SCATTERED SHOWERS."

Needless to say, we had the back-breaking job of cleaning the black oil from our boats, decks, shoes, clothes, not to mention the engines, propellers, and the air scoops; the Germans had their final revenge. The civilians of Naples had a massive clean-up job also. Their city was devastated. The Germans had mined their water and gas lines, which left gaping holes in the streets, and the resulting craters made the streets impassable. Civilians poured from their homes to help the Allied liberators, and our American soldiers manned bulldozers, picks and shovels to bring life back to the city.

We boarded some German prisoners for transport; the ground crew from the Foggia Airdrome. They were dressed in all manner of soiled clothing, and we lined them up along the bulkhead. I tried to converse in my limited German, and was answered with a mean expression and nasty sounding words. They had been stripped and had nothing to share as a souvenir anyway. The damage to the city was disgusting, and we were glad to leave the harbor for the open water.

"SAT. OCT. 9, 1943 ON TO ORAN."

Our small convoy of transports left the congested harbor of Naples to pick up more cargo at Oran. The air was fresh and clear of the smell of oil. We felt we had done a good job in Naples, and the convoy plodded on its way. The destroyers took their escort positions, and the USS *Buck* was up ahead of our transport as usual. Then with the suddenness of a lightning bolt, the destroyer blew up into the air in a burst of fire and sank right before our eyes. Our moment of peace was shattered in the blink of an eye, and we scrambled for our battle stations, fearing that at any moment our transport could be next. The German U-boats had infiltrated our convoy, and our destroyer escorts were dropping depth charges with the steady booming and splash, which continued until finally all was clear, and we proceeded to Oran without further trouble.

"SUN. OCT. 10, 1943 CAME INTO ORAN THIS AFTERNOON."

"TUES. OCT. 12, 1943 WENT ON LIBERTY WITH RED AND GEORGE TODAY. SAW *WHITE CHRISTMAS*."

Red and George were always good company, and it was always best not to go into town alone. There seemed to be more people and more servicemen in the streets. We could not resist rousting out a few sleeping Arabs, and we got dirty looks and a few choice words in return. There were more Arab women walking in the streets in small groups of three or four, with their white robes trailing in the dirt. The dress on one in the middle of a group looked a little familiar, and Red said, "That looks just like one of our mattress covers." We fell in behind them and sure enough, it was a USN mattress cover, and on the bottom near the hem was the Navy stencil. We got the best laugh of the night; right there in big, black, bold letters, "A. J. Smith, USN." During the remainder of the evening the conversation centered on our speculation as to how the mattress cover got in the hands of the Arab woman. We ended the night still laughing, watching the movie *White Christmas*, which we had seen many times over.

"WED. OCT. 20, 1943 SENT HOME $75 TODAY, WHICH MADE $300 IN ALL."

"MON. OCT. 25, 1943 LEFT ORAN TODAY WITH TROOPS OF THE 1ST ARMORED DIVISION. EXACT DESTINATION UNKNOWN AS YET."

The assembly of ships in convoy # NSF-6 arrived in Naples, Italy on Thursday, October 28, 1943.

"FRI. OCT. 29, 1943 UNLOADED TROOPS AND CARGO IN SIX HOURS, JUST ABOVE NAPLES. GOT UNDERWAY FOR ORAN AT 5:00."

"Sun. Oct. 31, 1943 Halloween, it seemed so remote. Arrived in Oran today. Some good rumor going around that we may be going home!!"

"Tues. Nov. 2, 1943 Election day at home and Aunt Mabel's Birthday. Started loading scrap metal today. Assured now that we are going home to the states."

"Wed. Nov. 3, 1943 Received Ann's package today, it was swell. Made me homesick for her."

"Thu. Nov. 4, 1943 Finished loading scrap today and preparing to load casualties. It won't be long now."

"Sat. Nov. 6, 1943 Left Oran at midnight to get underway for the good old U.S.A."

"Sun. Nov 7, 1943 Entered Straits of Gibralter about 4 P.M. today. Came into the Atlantic around 9:00."

"Mon. Nov. 8, 1943 Entered the Harbor of Casablanca at noon and docked about 2:00 P.M."

Our ship nosed in the harbor carefully, for there were small fishing boats everywhere. Fishing seemed to be their lifeline, and they spent most of their shore time making and mending huge nets. They did not seem to get much help from the Arabs, for they never seemed to be doing anything but resting.

"TUES. NOV. 9, 1943 WENT ON LIBERTY TODAY. PRETTY NICE CITY."

We loaded a few more wounded today, and were about filled to capacity. Like kids out of school, we dressed for liberty and invaded the town. We had heard about Casablanca many times; it was a beautiful city with many parks and palm trees. In front of the Banque Nationale, there was a crossroads sign with mileage to Washington 4,900 miles, Tokyo 10,200 miles, New York 4,600, and Berlin 2,500 miles. We found a mixture of servicemen at the Anfa Hotel, and we were all ready to celebrate. Soon we found our way to some action. The beer was strong, and we were fairly juiced in a short time. There were some French people mixed in with the servicemen, and one of our group, a bit unsteady, got his eye on a French girl seated at a nearby table. Before we could stop him, he had gathered her in his arms and tried to kiss her. He leaned over and gave her plump bottom a pinch, and pandemonium set in. Her silver-haired, goateed partner protested loudly and called for the MPs. In no time at all the MPs had him by the collar, out into the street, and headed for the brig. I was right on their heels, and proceeded to act as negotiator. After talking for a few minutes, I found out the MP was from Alexandria, Virginia, too. When I promised to take care of our shipmate, he left him in my custody.

With the best of intentions, we headed back to the ship, when a street urchin approached us with good news. "Hey, Joe, come see beautiful sisters, you like." I guess you know we stupidly followed the little bugger through dark alleys, over walls, and through the back yards of homes until a pack of barking dogs brought us to our senses and we grabbed him by the neck and gave him a kick or two for leading us away from town. Now we were lost in the Devil's Kitchen. How we found our way back without being robbed or getting our throats slashed, I'll never know. I'm sure if we had become separated, as was his intent, it would have been a different story. We were lucky; we got back to the ship with our lives and money in our pocket. It was nice to be "in" with the cooks, and we consoled ourselves for our stupidity with a platter of steak and eggs. What a treat. Farewell to Casablanca!

"Wed. Nov. 10, 1943 Got underway for the States at 10:00 A.M. today."

We picked up our convoy of ships numbered TG27.4 and headed out into the Atlantic. It was reassuring to see the cruiser *Philadelphia* among our protectors. The German submarines were still tracking the convoys with alarming results, and it was back to battle stations and calls for general quarters. I was still working in the galley and was not on deck as much as the earlier crossing. This was a little more calming, for what I could not see, would not send my poor nerves quivering. Working around food has a calming effect, at least for me. When I wasn't on my watch, I was dishing out food or making delicious cocoa for the crew. The secret … a pound of butter in the pot to make up for the absence of fresh milk.

"Sun. Nov. 21, 1943 Arrived in New York Harbor today. Docked at Pier 20, Staten Island."

On Sunday, the *Elizabeth C. Stanton*, AP 69 troop transport with amphibious crafts and wounded aboard, arrived in New York Harbor. Ship horns and whistles blasted their salute as the mother hen *Lizzy*, with her landing craft (chicks) loaded close to her sides, steamed into the harbor with a giant salute and cheers for our "Lady Liberty." Flags of all sizes were flapping in the chilly breeze. We were all cheering and crying at the same time, making an enthusiastic, happy din. The martial music seemed to elevate the cheers from dockworkers and families gathered to welcome the walking and the wounded.

The Italians had surrendered, and the Germans had been driven from Africa and Italy. The ship was proudly displaying the European theater colors with battle stars for Africa, Sicily and Salerno. Our battle-scarred ship nosed her way through the harbor traffic of escort ships, sweepers, oilers, merchant vessels and fire tugs saluting our entrance with their hoses spraying a fountain. There was not an inch of room on deck; officers, chiefs, crewmen, cooks, walking wounded and those on stretchers were all there. Home at last, and what a sight … the

Red Cross wagon with coffee and donuts.

Debarking was painfully slow. Everyone was anxious to touch ground, but the wounded needed special care and it seemed an eternity before the ship was cleared.

We left the dock and moved on to the Todd Shipyard in Hoboken, New Jersey. My heart was pumping madly. I was almost home. Birthed next to our *Lizzy* was a ship being outfitted as a transport. We watched as they removed the name of *Sea Carp* and replaced it with the name USS *Clay*. It was obvious that the ship would need amphibious craft also.

While waiting for extended orders, we went ashore, and the phone lines were jammed with calls to moms and sweethearts. We caught the ferry and the subway to good old New York City, and thanked God we were back safely on American soil.

"WED. NOV. 24, 1943 WENT HOME THIS AFTERNOON FOR FIRST TIME IN 10 MONTHS."

A 24-hour pass; I was floating on air. Home, home at last! Everything seemed a little different, but then, I was different. I had gotten married, joined the Navy and been to hell and back.

I wondered if my dog King would remember me. What a foolish question. He wagged his tail so hard his big body was almost bent double in greeting. He probably thought I was back again to take him for long walks by the lake, or to chase rabbits down the old mill road.

I only had a short time, but it was lonely, for all my friends were in the service and our church bulletin had a long list of names and addresses.

"SUN. NOV. 28, 1943 GOT A SHORT LIBERTY AND WENT HOME (FOR THE DAY)."

We were all on edge waiting for definite orders; surely we would be given a little time for R&R. I dashed home to see the folks, but had not seen Annie yet, and I was chomping at the bit. On top of that, I had a feeling of unreality, the continual stress of fear had taken its toll, and I could not shake the dark apprehension for the future.

"Tues. Nov. 30, 1943 Left the *Stanton* today for Little Creek."

The *Stanton* needed a lot of repairs and a general overhaul, so our crew got orders to pack up and leave the *Stanton* and report to the Little Creek Amphibious Training Base. They boarded us on a train, and we were on to Virginia; at least I would now be closer to Ann.

"Fri. Dec. 3, 1943 Started on 15 days leave today. Got in Alexandria 7:30 P.M."

Every mode of transportation was filled with servicemen; trains, buses and automobiles. The Washington, D.C., area was especially congested, because of Fort Belvoir, Quantico, Norfolk, and the many departments of war. I finally arrived at Ann's house in Alexandria about 7:30 P.M.

It was different at Ann's house without her father, an old Calvary veteran of the Spanish American War, for he had passed away on October 28, at the time our convoy was loading for the invasion of Italy. I had not received any mail, but I was not too surprised, for he had a bad stroke at the time of our wedding.

Ann's house was like Grand Central Station; her mother was boarding two trainer pilots from the Hybla Valley Auxiliary Airport across the street. Also with her brothers at home, and Calvin preparing to go into the Army, we decided to leave for my home in Wenonah. The next day, Sunday, we took the train for New Jersey.

"Mon. Dec. 6, 1943 Home."

Peace and quiet at last and a chance to unwind in my old clothes. Home, why had I never realized how wonderful it was? My two pussycats ignored me for being away so long, but finally gave in and curled up on my lap. I unpacked my sea bag, which I had hastily dumped on my first trip home. It all seemed so unreal; the spoils of war spread out on my mother's spotless bedspread. The Italian helmet, the German bayonet, knife, fork, spoon and can opener kit, French and Italian paper money and coins, leather purses from Africa, and the bullet from the stomach of a wounded Carolina boy.

Why had I collected all this stuff? But then, my room was full of stuff I had collected through the years.

Time was slipping away, and there was barely ten days left. Ann and the folks insisted I have my picture taken in my uniform. I was a little put out that the tailor had not been able to sew my new rate on my uniform. After the invasion of Sicily, I had been promoted from Fireman 1st class to Motor Machinist 3rd class. Anyway, I pinned on my European service ribbons, with the battle stars, and posed for posterity. So glad I did; I will never be that young or innocent again.

"Fri. Dec. 17, 1943 Left home at 9:00 P.M. Caught train at 10:30. Said goodbye to Ann and the folks."

There is a certain sick feeling that you get at parting, which you never forget. It is a dread and a loneliness that sinks into your heart and it starts at the very second of separation. We waited on the train platform as long as we could, and I wondered if I would ship out before the Christmas season. It was hard to believe there was a season because of the blackout. Any decorations with lights had to be hidden indoors. Train platforms are the coldest places in the world, but we had that last hug and kiss and I made a mad rush to get on board.

Ann stayed with the folks until Sunday. She told me she was the only girl on the train going home, and it was so drafty and cold the snow blew through the cracks in the windows. She tried to sleep with her fur coat pulled up, and when she awoke at Washington station, she had two army coats piled on her, and I thought, *What, no Navy?*

"Sat. Dec. 18, 1943 Arrived at Little Creek ATB at 10:00 A.M."

"Wed. Dec. 22, 1943 Left Little Creek at 5:00 P.M."

Our orders finally came through. The amphibious crew was given orders to report to the USS *Clay*, a transport. It was the same ship we saw being outfitted at the Todd Shipyard. I had felt a strange feeling that an amphibious division would be needed, and now I knew it would be ours. I gave a silent sigh, for the *Lizzy* was a grand lady, and she had captured my heart. Our amphibious crew was on the move again, and we boarded the train for New York.

"Thu. Dec. 23, 1943 arrived in New York this morning. Went aboard the USS *Clay* APA-39."

The ship was in a turmoil of repairs, and we had to pick our way through the decks. I was thinking, *I hope they don't ship us back to Little Creek again*. We were surely in the workers' way as we shifted lumber and cables to get to our bunks, but we settled in as well as we could.

"Fri. Dec 24, 1943 Got a 36-hour leave and went home. Met Ann in Philadelphia."

Home for Christmas, the best news yet. I had a feeling that they wanted to get us out of the workers' way and I was not surprised (but pleased) to get a 36-hour leave. I called Ann on the phone and she was in Philadelphia waiting for me. The folks were overjoyed, and put up all the Christmas dressings, even my Christmas tree house, barn and trains. There was a wreath on the front door with the service flag and star placed in the middle.

The folks had the Woodbury newspaper with an article about my return.

WITH UNCLE SAM'S FIGHTING FORCES

William C. Stein F1c has returned to Norfolk, Va. after spending a 15-day leave with his parents Mr. and Mrs. William H. Stein of Elm Street, Wenonah. He returned to the States November 23, after spending over six months in the Mediterranean area, during which time he participated in the invasion of Sicily, and Salerno, Italy. During his last two months overseas, he made several trips to Naples, being the first Allied convoy to enter the port after its occupation by our troops. While in North Africa he met his friend and neighbor, Cpl. William S. Allen, who is now somewhere in Italy.

"Sat. Dec. 25, 1943 Spent Christmas Day with Ann and the folks."

"Fri.. Dec. 31, 1943 Spent evening with Ann at home. My last visit with the folks."

"Sat. Jan. 1, 1944 New Year's Day left New York for Norfolk, Va. on USS *Clay*."

I fell asleep on the train trip back to New York. The excitement of being home again with Ann and the folks left me shaken inside. Everything seemed to be moving in slow motion. All of our boat crew finally found their way to the Todd Shipyard in Hoboken to board the *Clay*. This was the same ship birthed next to us when the *Stanton* returned to the states. There were welders and repairmen busy converting the vessel for naval transportation service. The former name *Sea Carp* was removed and the ship was commissioned the USS *Clay*, under the command of Captain E. W. Abdill, United States Navy.

Workmen were still onboard as we wormed our way to our quarters. They had a lot more work to do and we could hardly sleep for the pounding and sawing going on. Our new landing craft were hoisted aboard, some were made by Higgins, Owens, and Chris Craft; but all companies used the Higgins design, and we were glad for the new replacements.

In spite of the unfinished work, we set sail for the NOB, Norfolk, Virginia. I noticed many new hands aboard, but most of our 3rd amphibious task force were seasoned sailors who had weathered several amphibious landings.

To say farewell to the Statue of Liberty is not joyous like saying hello, and we all stood on the outer deck waving a quiet goodbye. I'm sure I was not the only one wondering where our new ship was going to take us.

"Sun. Jan. 2, 1944 Arrived in NOB Norfolk today."

We were back at the Navy Receiving Station and barracks again. At least we are in Virginia, with the possibility of being able to call or visit Ann in Alexandria. The workmen were still on board, and we had a lot of work to do on our new boats. The crafts needed to be checked and refitted; the davits adjusted, and even some number painting to do. In spite of the workmen on board, we lowered our boats and managed to get in some trial runs to check and recheck our part for the amphibious landings. The sea mists were freezing cold, but we had to prepare for the troop maneuvers on the Chesapeake Bay.

"Sun. Jan. 16, 1944 Letter from Captain Dierdorff, USN."

Our crew had an interesting surprise from the captain of the *Stanton*. On January 13, 1944, he forwarded to our home address 82 7x5 pictures, taken by the ship's photographer, of all the ports of call in our European invasions. Enclosed with the pictures was a letter from our captain.

January 13, 1944. These photographs are sent to you as a gift of the ship for your loyal and efficient work

R. A. Dierdorff.

Captain, US Navy, Commanding.

"Thu. Jan. 20, 1944 Liberty to D.C. and Alexandria, Va. Spent the evening and day with Ann in Alexandria and Washington. Went up with Jimmy and Woody."

The liberty was short, but we pushed with the crowd. At least I had Jimmy and Woody with me. We met Ann and spent the day in Washington taking pictures and touring the monuments. The boys were looking for girls, and there were plenty in Washington. Ann rounded up two girls from work, and we were off to a nightclub for the evening. It was a bad idea; for one thing, the boys were not drinkers, they were still suffering from the trauma of combat, and with the second drink—myself included—we were feeling no pain. The packed dance floor made matters worse, and we were quite unfriendly with some "civilians" who made the mistake of stepping on Woody's foot. I was afraid of a free-for-all, especially with the girls there, so I suggested we go to another club. Ann and I headed down the steps, and Woody's girlfriend tried to help him. He was more than a little sloshed by this time and missed the top step. He rolled up in a ball, dragging her with him, and landed at our feet. Both girls were really mad, and left without even a thank you for a lovely evening. I did not get to spend much time with Ann, and it was a mad rush to return to the base on time.

"Fri. Jan. 21, 1944 Got back to the ship this morning. Guess Ann is mad at me after last night."

Speaking for myself, I was dead tired the next morning. There was work waiting for us at the dock; tons of ship's stores and equipment to stow away in the hold. The infirmary was distributing Adabrin tablets to the crew, and you did not need to be Einstein to figure we must be preparing ourselves for a tropic zone. I thought we could be going to France, but this new situation changed my mind. No matter where the ship was going to take us, our crew was sure to be in action again.

"Sun. Jan. 23, 1944 Called Ann tonight, was good to hear her voice again, miss her a lot."

I'm glad that Ann was not mad at me. I wouldn't blame her much. We were all kind of crazy thinking about what lies ahead for us. We had liberty in Norfolk again, and we had a feeling it would be our last for a while. There were white sailor caps and uniforms everywhere. All the stores and bars were filled to overflowing; there was not much to do. They served the beer in monstrous mugs, and soon we were feeling no pain. It was quite a sight, all young boys, so far away from home, and the future uncertain. Finally I got my turn at the telephone to call Annie, and by the time I got to the phone I had consumed my third mug and I'm sure she could not understand a word I was trying to say; I guess she thought we had a terrible connection. My buddies were in worse shape than I was and couldn't even remember whom they were going to call. Finally we knew we had to return to the ship, but we were turned around and lost all sense of direction. We walked on and on and could not seem to find where our ship was docked. We sat down, and I do remember it was late ... about 3 A.M. I could not seem to focus my eyes on the watch my father had given to me, but I could tell it was late. At last we all agreed to seek help. An angel must have blessed the man who answered the door to our frantic pounding, for he kindly steered us in the right direction. I remember thinking that I must stand up straight, and not look bombed when we go aboard. I saluted the flag smartly (so I thought), and then the officer of the deck. Jimmy and Woody did not do so well, but with our arms around each other we finally bunked in safely. It was to be our last liberty in the States for a very long time.

"Tues. Jan. 25, 1944 Loaded with marines today at NOB."

The tough marines of the 39th Replacement Battalion boarded on the double with their packs and armament. Their jeeps congested the deck, leaving little room to move, and we worked at a feverish pitch the better part of the day and into the night. We were so loaded I thought we wouldn't need a hit to send us to the bottom. In fact, the side view of the ship was a mass of equipment, above and below the bulkhead. Besides the crew, troops, landing craft, a jeep, lighters, booms fore, aft and amidships, life rafts, cargo nets, gun tubs, radio antennae and wind meters, the stack and superstructure were barely visible. Only our beautiful American flag waved free and clear of all the equipment of war. The showers were packed again, and we learned to take a bath in a bucket, or spend the day waiting in line to find the water had run out. Bathing wasn't the worst problem; the mess hall was getting triple duty. The tables were raised by removing pins on each side, and everyone had to stand to eat. In this way more troops were fed in a shorter time. Oh how we missed our private dining room on the *Stanton*.

"Wed. Jan. 26, 1944 Left NOB Norfolk today 6:30 A.M. Headed for the Panama Canal."

We were back out in that treacherous Atlantic again. Just like magic the turmoil started in my stomach, that short R&R hadn't helped much. Although we hugged the coast it was no insurance against the U-boats. The transport USS *Chase* was behind us in the convoy and it provided some comfort, because I knew some of the crew on board. The weather was warmer as we passed Florida; we had been following the zigzag pattern from the start, but now we had been called to our battle stations and I knew this meant the German submarines were watching our convoy.

"Sat Jan. 29, 1944 Passed by Cuba this afternoon; also Haiti, then entered the Caribbean Sea."

The water was a beautiful blue color, and Cuba so close it looked to be about sea level, but we noticed several groups of elevation. Our destroyer escorts were dropping depth charges, and the constant booming kept us on edge. On January 30, we passed the San Salvador lighthouse in the Bahamas. That night everything was quiet on deck; I was at my battle station searching the waves for the enemy. The coast was in complete blackout darkness; it was then I saw it. The Southern Cross, in all its ethereal beauty. An aura of light seemed to surround me, and for a split second I lost the focus of my vigil. Was the cross an omen? If so, good or bad? I shivered alone in the darkness.

"TUES. FEB. 1, 1944 ENTERED THE PANAMA CANAL TODAY AT 11 A.M. DOCKED AT 9 P.M. ON THE PACIFIC SIDE AT BALBOA."

There was an air of great apprehension and excitement as we entered the Canal Zone. I had the gun watch port side forward, for U-boats had been sighted in and around the entrance. The giant locks were under heavy guard; this great canal was the lifeline to the Pacific war. The "big ditch" as we called it, saved a lot of time and many man hours.

No words can properly describe the awesome sight of the canal. The massiveness and the amount of cement work are unbelievable. Warships were formerly designed so their width did not exceed that of the canal. However, the *Clay*, with its fat-sided amphibious craft aboard was far too wide for the locks. Consequently, our landing craft forward were lowered into the water. The cooks sent us off with a bag lunch, a huge pot of coffee, and the usual bologna sandwich. I won't mention the Navy's pet name for bologna.

There was an officer and crew for each boat, and we followed the giant transport through the three sets of locks. At Gatun, three double locks raised us 85 feet above sea level. As the water rose, I saw a panoramic view of unexploited forests, dense foliage, banana trees, and colorful tropical birds with large hooked beaks. An artificial lake was formed from the river, and the huge Gatun Dam controlled the lake level for the locks.

At Pedro Miguel, the ship was lowered to a large lake and there were two more double locks. It took a war for me to see this wondrous sight, and with a little feeling of braggadocio I thought, not many people in this world have crossed the Panama Canal in a thirty-six-foot landing craft; it was an unforgettable experience.

At 9:00 P.M. we reached the Pacific Ocean at Balboa, where some lucky sailors got a short liberty. So far the ride through the canal had taken about ten hours.

"WED. FEB. 2, 1943 LEFT CANAL ZONE TODAY

FOR PEARL HARBOR."

Out in the open sea at last. Without the danger of mosquitoes and malaria, I moved my blanket from below, to my landing craft on deck. The other landing craft above sheltered me from any tropical showers, and I felt lucky to have a private place where the stars and moon seemed close enough to touch. If general quarters sounded I was already on deck and close to my battle station. Pearl Harbor seemed like it was a long way from home and I wondered if we would have liberty to see the sights I had only read about and seen in pictures.

"TUES. FEB. 15, 1944 GOT SEVERAL LETTERS TODAY INCLUDING PICTURES FROM ANN AND CARDS FROM AUNT MABEL WHEN WE ARRIVED IN PEARL T.H."

The name *Hawaii* brought a picture to my mind of palm trees and hula girls, but the vision soon faded when we passed the carnage of Battleship Row. The harbor was a real mess. Since the attack December 7, many of the ships had been removed, but the *Arizona* and the *Oklahoma* were sad memorials of how unprepared we were. There were printed signs in the water to remind all where ships and men had been blown into oblivion on that fatal Sunday morning.

As soon as we docked, the mail was brought aboard and I received several letters at mail call. Ann sent the pictures we took when I was on leave. On one picture of me, Jimmy and Woody in front of the Washington Monument she wrote, "Three handsome sailors."

Ann sent a Valentine. On the big red heart was written: "Darling, may you always want to be my Valentine. Love, Ann." The card from Aunt Mabel said "Happy Birthday to a nephew who is serving our country." The picture on the front was a big flag shield with Uncle Sam's hat and a saber and the word *Victory*. The birthday card from Ann had a birthday message "To my husband in the Navy." The picture was a destroyer with a huge eagle hovering above it.

We worked at a steady pace all day unloading the 39th Marine Replacement Battalion, and all their gear and supplies. We scarcely had time to eat. This unloading was quite a maneuver since we were anchored at a buoy. Our boats had the duty to ferry all manpower, equipment, supplies, jeeps and mail to shore.

With the marines off the transport, the ship was ours again. No more waiting in long lines to take a shower only to find out the water had run out. We did not have our own dining room like on the *Stanton*, but they put the pins back in the tables and we could sit down to eat.

"Wed. Feb. 16, 1944 Was 22 years old today. At this rate I will be an old man when I get out of the Navy."

This will be my second birthday away from home. When I thought of all the wonderful birthdays in the past, I had a flash of that old homesick feeling, and I had to keep busy. I field stripped my guns and put them back together. My family had been gunsmiths and had supplied the Philadelphia Police Department, and this gave me a little comfort. I spent the remainder of the day cleaning and greasing my boat engine. Happy Birthday to me!

"Thu. Feb. 17, 1944 First liberty in Honolulu, bought several souvenirs."

You can believe there was a mad scramble to go ashore. I was lucky, for the port watch had the first liberty. The other watch had to wait until the next day. We were about seven or eight miles from town, and limo cabs holding about seven or eight passengers, were lined up at the gate. We passed the Aloha Tower, which we saw from our ship, and fields of crops, probably sugar cane and pineapple. The limo dropped us off at the famous "Hotel Street" in the shopping district. It was like a giant sea of white, as service personnel pushed and shoved their way through the streets. My first purchase was a flowered bathing suit for Annie. Of course I could not resist the beautiful satin pillow covers, with "HAWAII" printed across the front, for Aunt Mabel and the folks. Servicemen were not allowed to have cameras, except for ship's photographers, and we were anxious for some pictures. We finally found some pretty picture post cards to send home. There was a studio, and the line was so long we had to wait a long time, but we were determined to have our picture taken with the cute little Hawaiian girl to send home (not a brilliant idea). The line for the movie house was several blocks long, and after waiting for a few minutes, we were informed it was the line for the prophylactic chits so we left that in a hurry. The Army Medical Corps was far seeing to control prostitution and disease, for the marines, sailors, and soldiers outnumbered the residents of the island about 1000 to 1. Woody and I did not give the ordeal a thought (well, maybe one thought), but the vision of Annie with a meat cleaver erased it from my mind. That was the same day I almost got a tattoo; another bad idea.

The Navy had turned the Royal Hawaiian Hotel into a rest and recreation area for the wounded and battle weary. The beach was covered with barbed wire, which they sometimes rolled up in the daytime for swimming. Just to be in the glorious sunshine and feel the tropical breeze was like heaven, especially for the submariners who were so pale from months down below. Ships stores had set up cases in the lobby and we checked over the watches, but the watch my dad had given me was still in good shape. We played a game of ping-pong until we wore out our competitors, and then took a walk along the beach to the Alamoana, the only other hotel on the beach.

Martial law was in effect, and we all caught the bus at the YMCA and were back to the ship by six o'clock. This was the first of many liberties on the magical island, and their music has forever had a special place in my mind and heart.

We had heard rumors that we were to load up for an invasion on the island of Truk, but the rumor was followed by the good new that our Air Force fighters and Avengers dropped incendiaries and bombs, pounding the island and the Japanese ships in the Truk lagoon. Most of their large ships managed to escape, and the raid continued two days and one night. The enemy had been beaten down without land-based aircraft or amphibious invasion. Eniwetok was then taken without further resistance.

The news was received with a great sigh of relief for the island had a dreaded atoll reef 140 miles long, and would have been serious trouble for our landing craft.

"Fri. Feb. 18 1944 Left ship for a few days and went to Wapaio Point AOB Camp (Amphibious Operating Base)."

This morning our amphibious boat crew (all one hundred and forty,) were given orders to take our sea bags and board trucks for the amphibious operating base at Wapaio Point. Another newly assembled tent city, with the wood on the sides, and right on the beach. I did not question the Navy's reasoning, but it was truly a paradise. After settling in, we wasted no time heading for Honolulu.

"Sat. Feb. 19, 1944 Went on liberty in Honolulu again today. Bought some more souvenirs and went to a movie."

We found some beautiful pictures of Diamond Head and the Aloha Tower, and could not resist a picture of the big sign at the crossroads of the Pacific. The mileage to New York was 6720 miles; had we traveled that far from home? Manila and Australia were over 4500 miles, and it was quite certain we would be traveling in that direction soon. I agonized that we were not allowed to bring our cameras; the scenery was so lush and green, not to mention the hula dancers. Security was very tight, and someone's pictures could get into enemy hands. Picture backgrounds can reveal many secrets.

Food, other than the Navy's, was on our mind, and we headed for one of the little restaurants. The fried oysters were heavenly, and in my very first order I found a nice size pearl, but alas, it had been cooked and was black as your hat. I saved it anyway.

"Sun. Feb. 20, 1944 Came back to ship today from Wapaio Pt. One month since I last saw

ANN. MISS HER VERY MUCH. GOT TWO LETTERS FROM ANN."

We piled into the trucks today, and it was back to the ship, leaving the paradise of Wapaio Point behind. There was mail waiting for us and I read Ann's letters through twice, it was so good to hear from her. I was glad to hear that Ann had a promotion, and was now at a temporary building near the reflection pool. A walkway was built over the pool from the main building, providing more space and easier access. Also another plus, she was working in Ships Stores and she could follow our ship movements through invoices. Another plus, more money in our bank account.

"SUN. FEB. 27, 1944 GOT MAIL AND A LETTER FROM MY LITTLE SWEETHEART TODAY."

"TUES. FEB. 29, 1944 GOT TWO LETTERS TODAY AND LEFT PEARL HARBOR FOR GUADALCANAL."

Boarding the 22nd Marine Regiment and army replacements took the better part of the day, and we finally sailed out from Pearl. We were on deck when we passed Battleship Row, and a pall of silence settled over the ship; it was a stark reminder that our convoy was sailing into the unknown.

Our amphibious division had no watch while we were in port; that was the concern of the ships company, but at sea, our security made use of all hands, and rightly so. Our watches could change at any time and we were sent to places we were needed most.

We were only at sea a few days when the bosun piped for general quarters, and we scrambled for our assigned battle stations. Our armada of transports immediately assumed a zigzag pattern. A destroyer escort had picked up sonar echoes of a submarine in the area of our convoy. I had been through this before and spent about thirty minutes scanning the waves before the destroyer escort finally arrived. The booming and splashing of the depth charges began immediately, much to my relief, and after repeated dropping the submarine disappeared, and with a destroyer escort we left the convoy and proceeded on for a short stop at Funifuti.

The next night the seas became rough, and I left my blanket bed in my craft to bunk down with the crew. My bunk was down in the hold at the aft end of the ship. I missed the fresh air, but the enemy subs were in the area, and the call for GQ was constant. I was given the bridge watch duty to which I had never been assigned before. The bridge was the hub of activity and I was attentively fascinated by all the action at the heart of the ship. As I stood my post, I was surrounded by the soft murmuring of each officer efficiently examining charts and giving orders; the officer of the deck, the junior officer of the deck, the bridge communicator, and the quartermaster. The quartermaster sat on a high stool in front of a wide shelf where he recorded everything that happened in, on and around the ship, twenty-four hours each day for every day of the year. I was so interested my watch was soon over, but not before I noticed a definite thickening of the weather, and the crashing of the waves made walking on deck impossible. When my aching body hit the bunk I was instantly asleep.

Before I even started to dream my favorite dream, there was a loud crashing boom, and the ship shook so violently everyone was scrambling for the ladder. Someone yelled torpedo, and the hold was empty except for me. I was still groggy and half asleep, somehow feeling the alarm was just a crashing wave. I searched for my shoes. They were missing, and I had left them right under my bunk. I fumbled in the dark and finally found them, but they were definitely not mine and so small I could barely get my toes inside. Just when I thought I would sink with the ship, the boys were returning from the false alarm, and I found the culprit who was clomping around in my shoes. It was that Texan from "Corpus" and you could be sure he did not "borrow" my shoes again.

On March 4, our original orders were for an invasion of Kavieng, New Ireland, and we were overjoyed that the air and ship blockade had neutralized the area, and we continued our way to Funifuti.

"TUES. MARCH 7, 1944 MET BENNY FROM WOODBURY HIGH ON BOARD SHIP TODAY."

I passed an army officer on deck and recognized a high school friend from home. This was his first trip, and I felt like an old war veteran with the invasions of Sicily and Italy behind me. He had boarded with the replacement group to debark at Funifuti, for future orders.

"WED. MARCH 8, 1944 WAS INITIATED FOR CROSSING THE EQUATOR TODAY. I AM NOW A SHELLBACK."

There was some excitement below in the ship's company. Even at the time of war, the initiation was going to proceed as usual. Everyone who had not crossed the equator before was ordered to the main deck at the super structure. It was a mandatory order from King Neptune himself, and his Royal Court. I did not know what to expect, and I don't know where the crazy costumes came from, but there they were in all their royal robes. (Mop wigs, sheet robes, crowns cut from tin cans, and coconut shells in the right places for a whistle or two). We were reduced to our skivvies, and ran through a line of shellbacks, who urged us on to have our hair cut in great chunks, and then we were seated in a chair that was charged with a small jolt of electricity. After this action they moved us on to the King's Court, where our mouths were held open and our throats were sprayed with a flit gun containing vinegar and hot pepper. (For the new generation, a flit gun looked like a tin can with a pump attached. For household use, the flit gun contained a powerful fly killer, and was a housewife's first defense to combat contamination by flies.) Before we had recovered from the gagging hot pepper, we were dumped over backward into a 5x5 vat of water. The King's Court graciously retrieved the gagging, sputtering victims from the water to slather us with black grease from head to toe. We were now officially "shellbacks" and left to ourselves to clean off the greasy mess.

On March 10, we arrived at Funifuti and discharged the army replacement contingent. Funifuti is one of nine islands in a group of atolls at Ellis Islands. The atolls were another new experience for our amphibious group. This little island was very flat, and with the tide, we easily cleared the reef. After we debarked the army replacements, it was dark, as only a Pacific island can be at night. The tide had ebbed, and then we had some embarrassing moments. It did not take us long to realize we were hopelessly wedged on the reef; every time we tried to back up we just boiled up the sand. We hung our lantern over the side and poked around with our hook. We had to think of something before the new hands aboard could witness our embarrassment. Hastily, trying to look like old pros, we moved all gear and passengers forward, and backed off safely. This was only the first of many problems with the dangerous atolls of the Pacific Ocean. This lesson would serve us well, for had we misjudged the timing of the tides during an invasion, our small craft would have been an easy target for the enemy.

"Tues. March 14, 1944 Wrote Ann today."

V-mail to: *Mrs. William C. Stein, Rt #4, Box 447, Alexandria, Va., c/o Mrs. R. Scutt*

From William C. Stein MOMM 3/c, USS Clay, C/o FPO San Francisco, Calif.

March 14, 1944

Dear Annie,

At this time there isn't very much to write to you about, so I will use the V-mail. I'm sorry my letters were blanked out by the censor; I try to be careful. I have no idea when this letter will reach you, but hope it will be soon.

When you get this letter it will probably be a considerable length of time since you got my last one, and after this you may not get any more for a while. However, please don't worry as I am well, and everything is all right.

I will keep writing to you whenever I get the chance, which may not be very often. I haven't gotten any mail for about two weeks now, and I doubt if we will be getting any in the near future, so I will just have to hope that everything is OK at home. Take care of yourself,

and so long for now. All my love,
Bill

"MON. MARCH 20, 1944 TWO MONTHS TODAY SINCE I LAST SAW ANN."

"WED. MARCH 22, 1944 FINISHED DISCHARGING TROOPS AND EQUIPMENT AT GUADALCANAL TODAY."

The struggle for Guadalcanal had been over for more than a year. I had read about the fierce battle and the many ships, Japanese and American, that were sunk and beached between Guadalcanal and Savo Island. Because of the many disabled and beached ships, this strip of water was thereafter known as Iron Bottom Bay. The shoreline drops deeply, and ships were left in an unsalvageable condition; the bow stranded on the beach, and the stern submerged in a deep trench. This four-month battle was the 1st Marine Division's first beachhead, and it was a do-or-die mission, with Australia and New Zealand at stake. They fought furiously night and day through swamps and a jungle hell, all with meager air and sea support. It was here at Guadalcanal the amphibious doctrine of invasion was developed to push the enemy back.

The *Clay* entered Guadalcanal at Lunga Point near Henderson Field. The waters down the slot were cluttered with damaged and beached Japanese ships and barges. We passed the Japanese transport *Kinugawa Maru*, with its bow on the beach and the stern sharply submerged in the deep channel.

I was unprepared for the utter destruction. Palm trees blown apart and scattered, rotting life jackets, ammo cases, rusting artillery parts, rotting clothing, empty boxes, and the broken and rusted armament.

Our landing craft were lowered, and we started the unloading of troops and supplies, not stopping until all were ashore. The ship moved over to Tulagi, and we anchored on the river. With our boats in the water, we did small repairs and touch-up painting. There was a little fun time; we did taxi service up river to the base club, and picked up the mail. We were able to relax a little in the shelter of the river.

There were signs that we would be going back to Pearl, and I was all for returning to the beautiful island. It would mean we would be picking up new troops to transport back to the war zone.

"Sun. March 26, 1944 Two months since we left the States."

While in Guadalcanal Captain H. S. Thornhill, Commander Division 10 came aboard our transport.

"Sun. April 2, 1944 Dad's birthday today."

"Sun. April 9, 1944 Easter—Arrived in Pearl Harbor, T.H. today. Received nineteen letters."

Coming back to Pearl was a little like coming home. I felt safe and cool for a change, with the trade winds blowing. The tropical heat rash was driving us crazy, and just to take a cool shower helped. We were given some kind of ointment in the infirmary, but keeping the bandages on the groin area and armpits was a struggle; as soon as it cleared up we would be back in the tropics again. It took me all afternoon to read my letters, and I read Ann's over twice.

(Rec. April 9)

March 14, 1944

My Darling Husband,

Well here it is Tuesday night. Last night I went out with Ardel, a girl whose boyfriend is in Hawaii. We had dinner out and just talked about our men. He has been in Pearl Harbor since before the bombing. They were to be married that Christmas. It really makes me thankful that we got married first. He sent her a lot of beautiful things; satin pajamas, grass bag, slacks, shorts suits, and hose. Of course he has been away a long time. We went to the movies and saw Madam Curie. *It was a good show. We went to her apartment after* *and had a small glass of port, and looked at pictures, and of course talked of old times. The best event of the evening was when I went past a jewelry store and saw a lovely anchor pin in the window. Darling, darling, it is so lovely. It has little shiny stones all over. When I asked the price, $6.50, it was so expensive I felt bad, but, darling, did I tell you that someone stole (I think) my navy pin from my coat in the coatroom? I feel so bad because you gave it to me, so I knew I could spend $6.50 for a pin that I might always wear something to remind me of you; especially when I go up home. I want to wear it on my Easter suit. Ginny Simms is singing, "Good Night, Wherever You Are," so I bought the pin.*

Bea's niece is sick so we did not go to the show tonight. I'm just as glad because I went out last night. Mom and I went to church Sunday, and it rained, but we took the car and so did not get very wet. George promised to go with us next Sunday.

The home front morale went down flat after that big article concerning that American soldier who was father to quadruplets by an English girl, and also married to a girl in Pennsylvania. The girls in my office who have husbands in England sure felt bad. Their husbands are always asking for money, but after this, the girls all wrote their husbands that they would not send any money to spend on English girls. I guess they can't judge them all by one, but ...

Gee, honey, I'm being such a good girl, and no one to pat me on the back. Well anyway I still love you and glad that you send money home to me. I'm saving it.

Always and always,

Your Ann

P.S. Here is a big lipstick kiss, honey, and by the way, it is the Evening in Paris lipstick that you gave me for Christmas. This will have to do until the real thing, honey. I'm enclosing the material that I am covering the living room couch with. The chair is flowered material; that is all done and the couch is next. The lady next door wants me to show her how to make them. Now good night, darling, say a prayer for us, dear.

Love, Ann

Enclosed, a little note: *Mrs. Ann Stein's financial report to Mr. William Stein:*

As of February 28, 1944: Camden Bank—$700.00, Alex. Ntl. Bank—$677.00, Bonds—$575.00, Bonds—$400.00—Total $2,352.00, minus $6.50 for pin (just joking).

This, of course, is our combined effort. I think Aunt Mabel has another bond for you in her safety deposit box. At work I'm going to get a $50 bond every third payday instead of a $25 bond every second pay. I think I can make it if my increase of pay is in my next check. The Navy Department is paying me $2,100 per annum, and I should get another promotion in a few months. Remember also, darling, every payday I buy something for my cedar chest. I hope this pleases you, dear; above all I want you to have something nice to come back to (beside me, of course).

Tonight I received 2 letters from you dated Feb. 22. Your letters are really swell and don't think for one minute that I don't count on receiving letters as much as you do.

Love, Ann

The envelopes still smelled of Evening in Paris; just to inhale made me homesick. The other guys enjoyed it too. The Easter card from Ann had two flags on the front with Iris flowers all around. "Easter greetings to my husband in the service." There was a poem also.

Let's both remember the lovely Easter days we knew.
All the happy little things that meant so very much, too,
And Husband dear, at Easter, let's both look forward to
When the world will be at peace and we'll
Be together again!

(Rec. April 9) *Sunday 8:15 AM*

March 25, 1944

Dear Bill,

I'm listening to "I'll Get By, as Long as I Have You," in organ music on the radio. Darling, every word of that song is true. I will get by; we both will get by as long as we have each other to pray for and to love. Do you ever hear a radio? If so, where and what programs? I would like to listen to the same ones. Darling, it will be quite sad to eat my colored eggs without you, dear. It would be nice if I could go up home for Easter instead of Palm Sunday, but I just can't take it. Remember when Bill Allen, you and I went over to Mantua looking for flowers, and finally you bought me sweet peas. I will look forward to when we can be happy-go-lucky again.

The weather is perfect. I will wear my orchid suit to church this morning. The sun is bright and the buds are out on the trees. The cherry blossoms will be out April 5, so the paper said.

I'm as happy as a kid about going up home this weekend; I hope the weather is nice. Of course I will take the pictures of your buddies and us. I will tell them what nice pals you have, and I'm sure they will feel a little better.

It has been 18 days since I have had a letter from you, but I'm sure one will be coming soon.

Everyone looks at my little anchor pin and likes it very much. I would like it better if you had given it to me, dear.

Remember I love you,

Ann

Will I ever get home?

"MON. APRIL 10, 1944 GOT FOUR LETTERS TODAY."

"TUES. APRIL 11, GOT TWO LETTERS TODAY. WENT ON RECREATION PARTY, PLAYED BALL."

The Navy does take pity on us and sends us on a recreation party once in a while. At least in the islands we were not working hard.

We pulled anchor for maneuvers on the island of Maui to practice with divisions of the second and fourth Marines. The Marines with all their armament were battle ready, but now it was up to the Navy to show them how to get to shore safely. Landings on the Pacific islands were treacherous due to the coral limestone atolls surrounding each island. Some were wider than others, and some had channels of entrance, but in each case it was the responsibility of the amphibious crews to keep the troops moving safely. Their first few trips down the cargo nets into the landing crafts were always a disaster. After repeated trials, they were soon spilling over the side like ants from a sugar bowl. Working together with the other services built a bond, for we needed each other if we were to finish our job and get home …

Maneuvers on the island of Maui were a lot easier; the weather was so beautiful with the trade winds blowing. We anchored near the port of Lahaina. Behind the port, the beautiful mountain peak Haleakala rose in all its glory; the highest peak on the island. We walked up a dirt road to Lahaina. There was a little bar at the port with mementoes on the walls of the whalers from years past. The Post Exchange had some nice soft work dungarees for sale, and I bought several pair. Since they were bell-bottom, I felt like a real cool seasoned salt. Our shop on the ship was always out of stock and they only sold the regular GI issue. We did not see any whales, but there were lots of banyan trees with their large roots extending from the ground to the limbs.

"Thu. April 20, 1944 Three months today since Ann and I were together last."

"Wed. April 26, 1944 Three months since we left the States."

"Mon. May 1, 1944 Was promoted to MOMM 2/c today."

Good news. Lt. Whittican, Commander of L Division boat crews, called me to the mess hall. He had been with our amphibious group since Italy, and I had worked for him some. He knew I was a hard worker and kept out of trouble, but I wondered if I had done something wrong. He surprised me by telling me he needed me to take charge of the six-boat crew of twenty-four men. First I was to take the exam for Motor Machinist 2/c. He had good faith in me, and I passed the test (fortunately). I'm sure he was concerned with a group who were always sneaking off playing craps below instead of working, but together, in a very short time, we took care of that.

I was anxious to tell the folks and Annie the good news. I had been young and eager to serve when I joined up, not realizing my Navy Yard experience could have earned me a good rating right away; however, I have enjoyed my experience with the amphibs and the small boats, which are truly an essential part of every invasion.

"Tues. May 2, 1944 Ship went to the island of Hawaii today."

Hawaii, the largest of the Hawaiian Island chain was rich with volcanic soil. There were masses of mountains and fields of pineapples, sugar cane and coffee. The grazing cattle had lush fields to feed on. The troops were busy with landing maneuvers, and they seemed to feel we were about ready to ship out again.

"Sun. May 7, 1944 Went on liberty in Honolulu today."

It really felt great to be on shore again, and have a little change from work. I am sure all the other thousands of servicemen felt the same way.

"Tues. May 9, 1944 Went on a recreation party today, played ball."

"Thurs. May 11, 1944 Went on liberty in Honolulu today, saw the picture *Tender Comrade*."

"Sun. May 14, 1944 Left P.H. today for a few day's maneuvers."

"Mon. May 15, 1944 Today is Mom and Dad's anniversary."

"Sat. May 20, 1944 Four months since Ann and I were last together."

"Fri. May 26, 1944 Four months today since we left the States."

"Tues. May 30, 1944 Memorial Day, left P.H. Today in a convoy bound for Saipan in the Marianas."

The *Clay* was the flagship of the transport division; our destination Saipan. Control of Saipan would bring us one more step closer to Tokyo, and an airstrip there would give a longer range for our B-29 bombers. There were about seven transports in this enormous convoy, just in our division, and we took all the necessary precautions, for our charted course was very close to Japanese air and naval bases. The trip was fairly uneventful, except the dispatch from the ship's radio room on June 6, announcing D-Day for the Normandy beachhead. Our APAs were again in action on the shores of France.

"Wed. June 7, 1944 Arrived Eniwetok today, received 7 letters."

We were all glad to finally get a mail call. We were given a recreation party, with warm beer, but I was not much for beer and I shared mine with others. I was told the name Eniwetok means land between west and east. We had taken the island from the Japanese about six months before, at the cost of 339 Americans killed and 2677 Japanese. It was a very important staging point for the Army, Navy, and the Marine Corps in their progress to the west. There was no doubt in my mind that the convoy was just biding time for a D-Day of our own; the ship was filled to overflowing.

"SAT. JUNE 10, 1944 LEFT ENIWETOK THIS MORNING FOR SAIPAN."

"TUES. JUNE 13, 1944 ANN'S BIRTHDAY TODAY, TWENTY THREE YEARS OLD."

"WED. JUNE 14, 1944 TODAY WE HEARD FROM THE RADIO ROOM TOKYO ROSE MADE A TAUNTING BROADCAST TO THE TROOPS; 'WE ARE READY FOR YOU, GI,' SHE SAID."

This wasn't the first time that Tokyo Rose had broadcast news of our troop movements. She had a lovely speaking voice and played our American songs, trying to make us homesick, and she succeeded. Of course we did not have radios of our own, but we got some information from the radio room. We were so busy and tired, I don't know when we would have had time to listen.

"THU. JUNE 15, 1944 D-DAY! WILL ATTACK SAIPAN THIS MORNING."

Saipan D-Day, June 1; just the word *invasion* put my nerves in the danger zone and my stomach churning again. So far we had a reasonably peaceful trip, but as we neared the island there was no mistaking our objective. Intelligence had reported a heavy concentration of Japanese troops, armament, and aircraft in the immediate area. I had been extremely uneasy when we were told we were to invade by the light of day, and not at 3 A.M. as we had done in the European invasions.

Our day at sea had been clear, but as we neared the island, a great pall of smoke covered the rugged terrain. The shoreline seemed to rise in giant steps, and the great Mount Tapotchau could barely be seen above the smoke. We anchored about six miles out, and our cruisers and destroyers off shore were blanketing the beach and beyond with a barrage from their five and eight inch guns.

The Japanese from higher elevations were furiously defending their island with machine guns, mortar fire and continuous shelling. Even at our anchorage, the booming din was so great we could not hear our own voices.

There was a little change in our landing plans. Because of the fierce resistance, our wave of landing craft was needed to provide a fake diversionary landing at another spot on the beach. Perhaps this fake landing could draw the Japanese troops away from the planned landing area, and our wave was the bait!

We lowered our empty boats on the far side and conducted our circle maneuvers as though our troops were boarding, then headed for the spot of diversion.

The plan seemed to be working, for we soon heard bursts of machine gun fire, and shrapnel fell over our heads. The firing was more intense as we neared the reef. The communications boat was not far behind, and we checked to find out just how close to shore we were to go. We were hunkered down in our boats, for we noticed heavier armament was being concentrated in our direction. There is no other noise like the whooshing of a mortar shell, and we heard it. It was there upon us in a wink. The shell exploded and splashed over our bow, sending a great rooster-tail geyser into the air.

I had an instant flash of self-preservation (which had kept me safe so far), and I screamed to the coxswain to turn back. He was scared too, but he said, "The communication boat has not given orders!"

Anger jaded my fear, and I jumped at the wheel and gave him a blast. "If you don't turn around we will be dead, and I'm not going to get killed for a fake landing." The other boats were right behind us; I guess they got the survival message too.

The battle scene at the actual invasion site was just that, a battle scene. The barrage from our battleships was more concentrated than ever. Gunboats seemed to be everywhere, their 40 mm fire support pelting the persistent shore batteries. Planes and avengers, with rockets from the escort carriers, were swooping around strafing and pounding the enemy, which was entrenched in the high ground.

Hundreds of amtracs, loaded with marines were crawling to shore over the wide barrier reef. LVTs from Eniwetok had loaded them up and brought them over to lead the way inland. Unfortunately, some of the amtracs had been stranded on the reef, and marines struggled to shore without their protection.

It was late morning by this time, and the troops on our transport were ready to board the landing crafts. There was a strip of seasoned 2nd Division Marines, some of the untried 4th, and a squad of soldiers escorting a contingent of American Indians, and we wondered what the escort was for. (Later it was revealed that our communication was greatly enhanced by the Indian "wind talkers'" un-decodable messages sent and received in their native tongue.) They had been waiting and were ready to go, and as they scrambled down the cargo nets, we protected them as well as we could considering the constant barrage of mortar fire. We circled our crafts at the far side while waiting for all the crafts to be loaded, and although the assault was upon us, we proceeded to the shore as planned. We tried to keep some sort of a V pattern, but it was necessary to change our positions often. As we neared the reef we found there was only one channel through, and that was heavily covered with machine guns, mortars, and handgun fire. We backed off, and with the magic of communications, a charged explosion blew a giant hole in the reef, and the landing proceeded. The water was filled with debris, for the marines who preceded us had a bloody time of it. The amtracs were not equipped with a ramp for fast debarking, and they exited one by one, making them easy targets for the enemy. Amtracs are equipped to go on shore and carry troops inland, but the reef and resistance changed the plan to their disadvantage. We had no time for horror as our propellers thrashed their bodies about in the water; we were trying our best to keep from getting blown apart ourselves and get our men safely to shore.

The troops were on their knees and crawled their way through the shallow water to the beach. There were craters of sand, debris, and dead bodies everywhere, and I noticed to my horror that our engines were sputtering and stalling out. Some were broached and turned aside. Our element of speed was going out the window. What had gone wrong? We had never had this problem before and a hasty inspection discovered slimy, rotting masses of sea grass had clogged our intake scoops, which were big as hods, and had jammed the propellers. The sea grass had been uprooted by all the mortar shells and gunfire, and was collecting close to shore. This was bad news, for it meant we could not leave our engines running while the troops were debarking, making us targets for the enemy if our engines could not restart.

We scraped and clawed at the weeds to free the sea scoops, but every time we started the engines, we had to jump out and clean them off again. With fear as our fuel, we tripled our speed to avoid the line of fire from the batteries on shore. This unexpected action was really shaking us up because we had several wounded in our boats that had been hit in transit, and we were responsible for their speedy transport back to the ship.

In spite of the rough surf, the debris in the water, and the enemy snipers, we continued our landings as the marines struggled to get a foothold on the beach. The tenacious Japanese continued to hold the air strip, and at about 3 P.M., thousands of screaming Japanese soldiers, brandishing swords and bayonets, tried desperately to push the marines back into the sea. The assault was communicated, and our cruisers and destroyers opened up the sky with a shellfire that jarred the bones in your body. A fog of thick, black smoke now hung over the island like a shroud, and the enemy retreated.

Desperately trying to shore up their batteries, the Japanese garrison called for backup troops from the nearby island of Tinian. We spotted the rafts and flat transports as they tried to sneak in a back way. Each raft was so loaded they were floating deep in the water and they squatted down shoulder-to-shoulder hoping not to be seen. Had the situation not been so lethal, it would have been hilarious, and it was a wonder they did not capsize right there before our eyes. Our destroyers got the message and moved in once more to blow their flimsy boats right out of the water. There was a scramble to rescue some who were swimming, but they screamed in horror and swam out to sea to their deaths rather than be saved and taken prisoner.

The next night they repeated the same operation over and over with the same end result. Meanwhile, the marines were still fighting furiously night and day through swamps and through a jungle hell. When their iron rations ran out, they scooped up fish with their helmets, and ate them scales and all. They pushed on, drinking muddy water and mixing powdered eggs in their helmets.

Throughout the invasion, communications were maintained between our craft, the beach, and naval units off shore. Intelligence notified us that a fleet of Japanese planes was headed for Saipan. Their intention was to drop soldiers by parachute on to the beachhead. We were issued 45 automatics and armed with machine guns; we planned to lay prone in our landing craft, and shoot the invaders as they floated down.

We took our places in our boats; my heart was really beating triple time by now. I had survived the landings and loading all day, and now the enemy was going to drop down on my head. I remembered the old expression, "There are no atheists in foxholes," and I prayed as hard as I could, thinking about little Annie. I stretched out near the bulkhead, put my helmet over my groin, and waited for my doom. (The enemy paratroopers never arrived, thank God.)

The Japanese planes were intercepted, and our pilots dubbed the day as the Marianas Turkey Shoot. (408 Japanese planes shot down, 32 American planes lost.)

That night our ship had another close call. (I don't know how many more I can stand.) Someone, somehow, had left a hatch light uncovered in the hold, and I heard someone, somewhere yell "Here comes Washing Machine Charlie on the port side." The Japanese had seen the light and zoned in on the target … our ship. Three bombs hit near our starboard side, sending water gushing over everything, and immediately after, four hit across the port side, giving us the scare of our lives. Somebody caught hell for the exposed light, I'm sure, and I was left with the shakes again.

As the invasion progressed, the Japanese became more frantic. Many islanders, who had been hiding in the rocky caves fearing the Americans, chose to commit suicide rather than be captured and tortured as they had been told they would be. They climbed to the highest cliff for a mass suicide. We could see them standing there on the brink and then, some holding hands, jump to their deaths onto the rocks 800 feet below. Some were old men, women with babies in their arms, and soldiers. This was accompanied by explosions as the soldiers pulled the pins on their own grenades. The scene planted a memory difficult to forget.

We were still working when dawn lit up the area, and I went to the mess hall between trips to the beach. I stretched out on a mess hall table and fell asleep instantly, but it only lasted for a flash. I was jolted awake by a bombardment that shook the ship. I grabbed a sandwich from the table and was on my way back to the beach.

I was relieved when the air raids quieted down some, but we still had to contend with the barrage of fire that was coming from the higher elevations. The wounded were piling up on shore faster than we could take them back to the ship. We did our best to keep them out of the line of fire and give them some comfort. Our ship provided one doctor and four corpsmen to the LST serving as a hospital ship, and we doggedly retrieved our casualties as soon as possible.

Dead bodies of Japanese soldiers littered the beach, bloated and decaying as they floated in the debris of battle. Great green flies blanketed their bodies and were on everything. We did our best to keep the horrible flies off our wounded but it was a losing battle.

Unloading continued through the morning and each craft had its own zigzag pattern to avoid gunfire. The withering bursts of mortar fire dropped metal debris, causing cuts and bruises on our faces and arms. Several of our crafts had been beached, and we worked feverishly to repair them, for no damaged craft was to be left behind. There were several thatched huts near the beach, with the sides and back blown out. Personal articles were scattered about and there were several dead Japanese soldiers, who had apparently been using the shack for cover. By now I was inured to death, especially the enemy's, so I pushed one if the bodies with my foot, and a sheaf of pictures fell out. I stuffed them in my shirt, and slid his bayonet into my belt next to my knife. He wasn't going to need it any longer. His body gave a *poof*, and I raced back to my boat as though I was being chased, thinking that my greatest fear—not getting back home—was going to be realized right then.

There were several beached boats to take care of, and after we attached the towlines, we checked the engine again to see if it could be repaired on the beach. We were rushing, for at any time a plane could spot us. With a spurt of adrenalin, I lifted the heavy engine cover. Just at that moment a mortar shell hit the boat next to us with a concussion that snapped me backwards with the engine cover jamming me between the gunwale and the engine. I was stunned momentarily, and when I tried to move, the pain in my back and arm was so crushing I lost all feeling. I don't remember the return to the ship, but they hoisted me aboard in a gurney chair and hauled me to sickbay.

The doc put my wrist in a cast and gave me a pain pill for the spasm in my back. One thing I didn't need was a sleeping pill, for I had not slept for two days, and I passed sweetly into oblivion.

Many hours later I woke up to more pain pills and my arm in a cast. I checked the deck to see what was going on. The marines, as they advanced, were using a new weapon, a flamethrower. The Japanese were so entrenched in their caves our losses were mounting. The entire area had a greater pall of black smoke than ever, and the sickening smell of burning and decaying bodies lingered like the shadow of doomsday. The big green flies had invaded the ship. They were everywhere; in the mess hall, in our food, on the walls, in our hair and mouths. Finally at dusk the amphibious force weighed anchor, and headed out to open water where the big green flies were blown away.

The invasion of Saipan by the marines and soldiers lasted twenty-five days with heavy casualties caused by the persistent resistance from the enemy. The airstrip on this island became a major base for the B-29 bomber.

Major General Henderson and staff debarked from our ship and stayed behind to later govern the island of Saipan.

"Tues. June 20, 1944 Five months since Ann and I were last together."

"Fri. June 23, 1944 *Clay* departed for Eniwetok."

The open sea looked good to us, in spite of the continuing hazards from the enemy. As any sailor can tell you, the sweet salt air has a quiet, calming effect. That night I collapsed on my blanket bed in my boat; no smoke, no flies, no noise. How long I slept, I can't remember. In spite of my dirty, itchy cast and the pain in my back, we had worked continuously for two days and two nights under heavy fire, and the quiet was unbelievable. I slept like the dead until the bosun's mate piped, "Chow down for the crew." Surprise, even the kangaroo hash (we swore it was kangaroo meat), and the green powdered eggs tasted … well, we ate them. One good thing, with the troops off, the mess hall tables were lowered, and we did not have to stand and eat. I could hardly wait for shower time, for no matter how tired I was, I showered and changed for the evening. It would have been nice to just stand and let the water wash all the grime of battle from my body, but we were only allowed a few minutes to soap and a few to rinse. No amount of water could ever wash away the grime of battle from my mind.

Several wounded men in our sick bay died, and the captain announced a burial at sea. We were to dress for the ceremony for those brave men who had sacrificed their lives in the bloody invasion of Saipan. Each of the four bodies was carefully sewn in a canvas bag, with a heavy shell casing put inside to weigh them down. The American flag was draped over top, and six honor guards were on each side. The service was short, but meaningful, for our captain was a kind, gentle person. We all paid our quiet respects and then the honor guard folded each flag as the bodies were gently slipped into the waters of the Pacific, somewhere near the Marianas atoll.

Our landing craft took a beating, and the ship's carpenters patched them up as much as limited space allowed. We did all we could with the engines, but the scoops on some would have to be replaced. We heard rumors that the *Clay* had more troops and supplies to pick up at Pearl, and it would be great to be in Hawaii again.

"Sun. June 25, 1944 Arrived Eniwetok, received 12 letters."

Mail is such a treat! I received a picture post card from Mother and Dad. There were pictures of the Capitol, the Washington Monument, the White House, the Lincoln Memorial, and the cherry blossoms. There was also a note:

Dear Bill: To show you we were here with Annie. Wish you were with us. Having a nice time.

Love, Mother and Dad

Boy, if wishes could only come true!

"Mon. June 26, 1944 Five months since we left the States."

We now had a little mascot, taken on board at Saipan. Someone in the ship's company found a little Japanese dog wandering around in the debris. He was black and tan colored, with large paws and perky ears. He did not answer to any of our calls; I guess he was used to Japanese words. He had a sad little face, and the electricians named him Sparky. They built him a cute little doghouse with a canvas roof, and we now had something to smile about; a little touch of home.

Unfortunately, life aboard a war ship became too hazardous for little Sparky, and one day in the midst of a GQ call, he fell through an open hatch; he was just learning to answer to his American name. A pall of gloom fell over the ship, as his little light went out in our hearts.

We were quite familiar with Eniwetok. We had the mail run and ran some small errands. This was recreation to us, and enjoyable. It was not unusual for the bosun's mate to pipe instructions for me to bring the captain's boat to the gangway for transport. This was quite a compliment, for the captain always picked a neat crew to ferry him to his points of business. The coxswain and I were neat and tall, and brown from the ever-present tropic sun. In our whites we felt quite the seasoned salts. It was a pleasure to operate the captain's boat. The ship's crew had spent the long days at sea braiding a cover for the ship's wheel, and for the ladder to the wheel deck, adding Turks heads and patterns into the design. The boat was an old LCP with no ramp and it had plenty of power. The captain often visited other ships especially when in port, and we felt pretty special to be chosen. Also we received other benefits, and we knew it would mean a great night out. The captain always said, "Drop me off at the gangway, and tell the officer of the deck to give you dinner and see a movie on deck. When the movie is over, bring the boat alongside."

We boarded fifty or so Japanese prisoners in their floppy diaper underwear, a sure sign we were going back to Pearl. We had to keep watch over them day and night for fear they would commit suicide.

"Wed. June 28, 1944 Transferred from the USS *Clay* to the USS *Knox* at Eniwetok, Marshall Islands."

What a black day! Without warning my name was called with orders to transfer to the USS *Knox*. It just couldn't be happening! The *Clay* was my home now. It felt like I was being punished for doing a good job and I had been with many in my crew since Italy. I didn't have much time to feel sorry for myself, but the song, "Have You Ever Been Lonely, Have You Ever Been Blue," kept running through my mind.

To lift my sea bag was pain and misery, and I wondered how I had accumulated so much stuff. I thought, *My back will never feel better if I keep torturing it so*. Well, so much for a return to Pearl and a little rest.

My spirits were lower than ever when they piped me aboard the *Knox*. It was a transport and the silhouette, with the landing craft aboard, was similar to the *Clay*, but the camouflage paint reminded me of a great barnacled sperm whale; not at all easy to warm up to. I was more than a little disgruntled.

I soon found out that the *Knox* needed experienced amphibious men to train their new hands, and other amphibs, not my crew, had been transferred also. Amphibious operations were difficult and dangerous, but with instructions and well-ordered practice, they were easy and formidable.

"Thur. June 29, 1944 Saw movie *Beyond the Shadow of a Doubt* tonight."

We settled in and watched a movie on deck. Tomorrow the work would begin, and I'm sure we would have little time to do it in. Our training and experience served us well, and we put the new hands through the landing procedures. The next few days, it was practice, practice, and practice some more.

My bunk aboard the *Knox* was small, cramped and under a sloping stairwell, giving my tall frame and aching back a workout. To add insult to injury, I noticed that the *Clay* had loaded up for the return to Hawaii and I was not aboard.

Not everything was all bad. I soon found out that my lieutenant was supportive and fair, and the waves of homesickness for the *Clay* lessened with each passing day.

"Sat. July 1, 1944 Saw *Big Street* with Henry Fonda and Lucille Ball."

"Fri. July 14, 1944 Saw movie *Yankee Doodle Dandy* tonight."

"Sat. July 15, 1944 Left Eniwetok today at noon."

We spent the day loading supplies. The *Knox* was gearing up for something big; another island invasion? Judging by the type of cargo, I could tell it would be soon, but where? We pulled anchor at noon to pick up troops, and now the ship would be packed again with little room to move.

"Wed, July 19, 1944 Arrived off Saipan this morning."

Saipan lay broken and quiet now; it had that after-the-battle smell, but the marines had scraped great trenches and covered the dead Japanese bodies, to our great relief. We did not want to battle the big green flies again, or witness the carnage.

The embarking troops seemed to feel that the island of Tinian was to be our next objective, and there was little doubt that they were right.

"Thu. July 20, 1944 Six months since I last saw Ann."

"Mon. July 24, 1944 Attacked the island of Tinian this morning."

Our D-Day invasion of Tinian was more orderly. They say practice makes perfect, and we certainly had a lot of practice. By now we were very familiar with the treachery of the reefs, and carefully watched the tides. The same units who fought so tenaciously on Saipan, were prepared to forge ahead here on Tinian.

Our wave of boats again created a diversionary landing to throw the enemy off balance, and we were careful to keep our distance. Our landing was well planned, and the marines forged ahead like demons and secured the island before the week was out. The problems we had at Saipan did not materialize, and our landings proceeded like clock work. We unloaded in record time; our casualties were 389 killed and 1816 wounded, compared to Saipan, where on the first nightfall 20,000 troops landed, and one tenth of them were casualties.

"Wed. July 26, 1944 Six months since we left the States."

The taking of Tinian was just one more step on our road to Japan. With the landing behind us, I was sure we would now need to return to Pearl for more troops and equipment; at least that was my fondest hope. We had a brief stop at Saipan to unload and load more supplies.

"Fri. July 28, 1944 Left Saipan today."

I was so glad to leave Saipan behind. By now the initial shock had worn off, and the horror of the casualties and my many close calls returned so vividly I could hardly sleep. There was every indication that we were going to Pearl; I believed the *Clay* had made another trip, and was probably there. Maybe my luck would hold out and I would see my old crew again.

"Tues, Aug. 1, 1944 Got first mail today on the USS *Knox*."

It seemed like a lifetime since I had any mail. No doubt my mail had been sent all over the Pacific.

I had a little accident coming from mail call. I was coming down the steps, in a hurry of course, when I caught my watchband in the safety chain. My watch flipped from my arm and fell to the deck below. The watchcase was bent, but it was still ticking and everything else seemed to be OK. That watch was a part of me, and I hoped I could get it fixed before I returned home.

"Wed. Aug. 2, 1944 Left Eniwetok today for P.H."

We were on our way! If all went well and we did not run into trouble, we would be in Pearl in about ten days. That was wishful thinking, for we were on constant GQ alert, and our destroyer escorts were dropping depth charges with the constant *boom booming*, which kept us on edge. I was also excited and sent my whites to the laundry. I lifted buckets of seawater to the deck to soak and whiten my caps. Honolulu here we come!

"Thurs. Aug. 10, 1944 Arrived in Pearl today."

We could smell that glorious scent before we docked. The Dole pineapple plant was processing for shipment, and the thought of those juicy pineapples set my mouth watering. We docked near the plant and I stood on the top deck looking over the island, inhaling, and thinking how close to heaven it was, and how close to hell we had all been. I scanned the docking area for the *Clay*, but she was nowhere in sight. I had heard from the radio room that the *Clay* had a new skipper. Captain E. W. Abdill had been relieved by Captain N.B. Van Bergen. We still had some clean up work to do, but I sure wished I was back on the *Clay*.

While in port, the ship's company had watch and station duty, but the amphibious division had a lot of work to do on their boats. My boat was to me like my car back home; I kept it polished and repaired, even using clean cloth and dipstick oil to clean and polish the engine. We used heavy grease to cover the cables and wiring, which were exposed to the ravages of salt water. My back was hurting, and I sat on the engine cover to let the numbers I had just painted dry in the sun. The boat was rocking a little and gently nudging the ship. I looked up at the dock and noticed a petty officer watching me. Obviously he was curious, but I had never seen him before, and I did not give it a second thought. When the paint was dry, I secured the boat and returned to the ship.

The next day my lieutenant and I were summoned to the captain's mast. An officer on shore had put me on report for being off the ship and not at my duty station. I was stung by the accusation, and my lieutenant was ready for a battle. I was so angry I could hardly speak, but I did not have to. The lieutenant informed the captain in no uncertain terms; "This man has a fine record. He is not ship's company; he is in the amphibious force. He has seen action in Sicily, Italy, Saipan, and Tinian, and I daresay he has seen more action than anyone on this island."

The council dismissed the case in just three minutes, but it made me wonder what would have happened to me if the lieutenant had not been there to back me up.

"SUN. AUG. 20, 1944 SEVEN MONTHS SINCE I LAST SAW ANN."

We took on fresh supplies, and it was great to have vegetables and milk. Our work was about finished, and with cool showers the prickly heat (commonly called crud or jungle rot) was finally disappearing from our body and armpits. It was the curse of the tropics and would return when we returned to the humidity and the heat of battle.

We finally got ashore and headed for one of the little restaurants for some real food, especially bread without weevils baked in. Even the smallest restaurants had a hula show and beautiful music of the islands. We lounged at the Royal Hawaiian just like rich people, and then walked the streets of the city with all the other servicemen.

The shops along Hotel Street were busy with service customers. Ah, Hotel Street, where there was a myriad of interesting things to entice the paycheck right out of your pockets. The tattoo shop had a long line, and I considered a nice tattoo with the name of my ship; but which ship? The *Stanton*, the *Clay*, or the *Knox*? While I was considering, I remembered the sore arms I had when I got my fever shots, and I walked on. The various picture studios, with their cute girls to pose with, were second in popularity only to the Army's girlie houses, and the pro stations. I had only one thing on my mind; find a jewelry shop and get dad's watch fixed. We passed a little tailor shop, and there were several uniforms displayed in the front. Right away I knew I had to have a tailor-made uniform. The little Chinese tailor bowed and scraped as I entered, seeming to measure my height with his experienced eye. He indicated that he was from Hong Kong and did the finest work, with the finest material available. There was more dramatic demonstration about quality, which was unnecessary for I already had my mind set on the beautiful dark navy worsted I had seen in the window.

"Very cheapy price," he kept saying over and over, when I asked how much. "You very tall, take lots material," he said, all the while measuring me with his eyes. He brought a stool from the back, and after making a big production with a tape measure he announced.

"Very, very cheapy, forty dolla. You big man." I returned a few days later, very pleased that the finished product fit like a glove. The material was soft as silk, and the flare in the trousers was perfect. The collar and cuffs were lined with satin, but the only problem—dress whites were the order of the day in Hawaii.

I had not forgotten about my watch and was lucky that the jeweler had a case that fit. It looked almost as good as new, considering the beating it had taken since I received it.

"Fri. Aug. 25, 1944 Left Honolulu today for maneuvers on the USS *Knox*."

The new hands adapted to the landing craft like a duck takes to water, and they thought it was fun. Now they would show us how much they had learned. There did not seem to be enough hours in the day, and we were under pressure to finish training as soon as possible. Rumors were spreading that the Philippines would be our next objective. We tried not to get impatient with the new crew, but no amount of practice could make up for the experience we had in actual combat.

"Sat. Aug 26, 1944 Seven months since we left the States."

Our ship was back at the dock and I was on deck, when the executive officer from the *Clay* was piped aboard. I recognized Commander Archie Simonstad immediately, and knew the *Clay* must be anchored near. My heart skipped a few beats for I felt that Archie was coming to retrieve his team. Our amphibious group had performed with unusual teamwork, precision, and competitive speed. There would be other invasions and the *Clay* had her reputation to uphold, and I hoped with all my heart that I was right. There seemed to be some hold up; apparently the *Knox* was reluctant to give up on our experienced group, but Archie won out. The *Clay* was to make a quick trip to San Francisco, and we would board when she came back to Hawaii. Worse luck! I had missed out on another trip to the States.

It was not long before orders came through; the *Clay* was back from San Francisco with more troops and supplies.

"TUES. SEPT. 5, 1944 TRANSFERRED TO THE USS *CLAY* FROM THE USS *KNOX* AT PEARL HARBOR."

Glory day! The transfer papers came through. I packed my sea bag, which was getting heavier, with my back hurting and protesting. To make matters worse, the docking area was packed and I had to pass through three ships to reach the *Clay*. Every hatch seemed to get lower and lower, as I dragged my bag behind me. Finally I reached my destination. It was like going home … well almost. Back to more maneuvers and frantic preparations with the 96th Army Division. They were preparing for an invasion on Yap Island, in the western Carolina group. We wasted our time and energy, for the invasion was later cancelled, which was fine with me and everyone else, I'm sure.

However, nothing stays the same, and although I had only been gone a few months, which had included the invasion of Tinian, our group had been reorganized. I was now assigned to boat # 17, and had to bunk down with the ship's company. The firemen were a tough group of guys (they had to be). Ziggy, in the bunk just below me, had arms like oak trees and muscles you could not believe. I'm sure I seemed like young prey to him, and he was constantly sparring and giving me teeth-jolting blows on my arms. I had to grin and bear it. I will never forget Phil, who lost forty-five pounds of sweat in the boiler room, where the temperature is cool at one hundred degrees. He had dark brown eyes and hair, and sported a jaunty mustache. He was a real salt, and sang comical ditties to keep us from going crazy. These dedicated men of the ship's company were the heart and soul of the *Clay*, and I'm sure they were responsible in part, for the *Clay's* efficient reputation. The quarters were close, and the ventilation pipes brought in only humid tropic air. Some cut holes in the vents over their bunks, but it did not help much. (I missed my blanket bed in my boat.) There was a new crewman in our group. The heat was bad enough, but he smelled just like a goat. Out of necessity, the engine room solved their own problems. The odorous offender was escorted, feet not touching the deck, to the shower room. That was the day he learned just what soap and water was for. Problem solved.

With my new boat # 17, came a new coxswain, H.P. He had been with our group since Italy and he was a good-looking, pleasant, carefree guy from Carolina, and we seemed to make a good team. He liked spit and polish too, and soon the captain was calling for us to pilot his boat. This duty counted as good days in the Navy.

"Fri. Sept. 15, 1944 Left Pearl Harbor today, bound for the Marshall Islands."

"Wed. Sept. 20, 1944 Eight months since I last saw Ann."

I had a bit of bad luck today. Before I left for my shower, I placed my watch under the mattress of my bunk. When I returned it was gone. The room had been empty when I left, but someone had searched it and found my watch. It looked like I would have to go home without it, if I ever get to go home. I hoped it wasn't a bad omen.

"Mon. Sept. 25, 1944 Arrived Eniwetok, Marshall Is. today."

Received an anniversary card from the folks on the 21st. It took ten days to get here.

September 11
From: Mrs. Mary Stein
E. Elm Ave. Wenonah, N.J.
To: William C. Stein MOMM 2/c
USS Knox—APA 46
First Division C/o Fleet Post Office
San Francisco, Calif.
Dear Son:

There is a little package coming. It might seem like a funny anniversary gift, but we are giving you something for your home, and sending it to Ann, but we wanted you to know we did not forget you, which you should know we never will. Please let me know if there is anything special you would like for Christmas. Did you get the other package? It was candy, and Aunt Mabel sent one too.

Love, from Mother and Dad.

"Tues. Sept 26, 1944 Eight months since I left the States. Got two letters from Ann today."

Another anniversary coming up and Ann sent me a card. The picture looked like a scene from our living room at home. (Am I blue????) The card was signed, *To my beloved husband from your loving wife Ann.* There was also a poem:

My darling husband:

I don't know where you are, but I know this letter will find its way to you. I think of you constantly. If I haven't heard from you I know it is not because you haven't written or that you haven't been daydreaming of me. I can tell by your FPO address in what part of the world you are, but as that covers a very large section indeed, I can't beam my thoughts to you definitely. May your head rest easy on whatever it has for a pillow tonight. My love is yours forever.

Ann.

At today's inspection, a small crew from the control boat, temporarily assigned to the *Clay*, was lined up by rank opposite me on deck. I noticed a fellow in front of me had a watch just like the one stolen from under my mattress. I stepped over and asked to look at it. It was mine. I did not hesitate. I called to the executive officer and told him the situation, and I easily identified the watch as a Belmar, with a crooked number. When the officer questioned the fellow, he said he bought the watch from another sailor who sold it to him for $11.00. The ship's chaplain took $11.00 from the ship's fund and paid the fellow for the watch. I was sure glad to get my watch back, and was thankful not to have to go home without it. This watch sure has a history.

After lights out at night, our group spent time on the deck. Once in a while they would show a movie on the superstructure, out of sight, but many nights we just sat on the deck and talked. We were all young and lonesome for home, especially with the moon and the swish of the waves on the bow. It was surprising how many songs we remembered. At home Annie and I used to buy song sheets every Friday at the drug store and memorize the words. I seemed to know more songs than any of the others, and before long we were singing every night. As soon as the lights were out they would say, "Hey, Frankie, what songs are we singing tonight?" They called me Frankie after I told them about the Steel Pier in Atlantic City, where we met Frankie and the band and danced to their music. It seems like everyone has a beautiful voice at sea. If the Japs heard us, maybe they would think it was our secret weapon.

"THU. SEPT. 28, 1944 LEFT ENIWETOK THIS MORNING. TODAY IS OUR WEDDING ANNIVERSARY."

It has been two years since our wedding. It seems so long ago. I watched the stars and wondered if Annie was thinking of me. I finally had my boat in position on the deck so I could sleep there with my blanket. It felt so free to be topside again where I could feel the salt air.

"SUN. OCT. 1, 1944 TODAY STARTS MY THIRD YEAR IN THE NAVY."

"TUES. OCT. 3, 1944 ARRIVED MANUS IN ADMIRALTY ISLANDS TODAY."

Plans had been changed for an island invasion, and our ship needed to be adjusted accordingly. Troops and cargo were shifted, loaded, and unloaded to accommodate the destination change. At sunset, the PT base came alive as their multiple Packard engines thundered out to sea for their nightly torpedo run. There was one thing certain; we were loading to invade somewhere.

"SAT. OCT. 14, 1944 LEFT MANUS TODAY BOUND FOR LEYTE, PHILIPPINE ISLANDS."

Leyte seemed to be the logical step. It was in the middle of the Philippine archipelago, and it seemed that MacArthur was going to do everything possible to keep his promise to the Philippine people, and we were going to help him. It looked like in another four or five days we would be in another invasion, battling for our lives.

"FRI. OCT. 20, 1944 ARRIVED AT LEYTE, P.I. THIS MORNING, WHICH WAS UNDER HEAVY BOMBARDMENT."

The *Clay* was a part of the mighty convoy headed for Leyte, and the battle for the Philippine Sea. There was a ship traffic jam, to say the least. There were ships as far as the eye could see. Communications counted 738 ships, and 420 amphibs; the most powerful force ever assembled. There were two screens of destroyers hovering and protecting our transport group as we moved toward Leyte. Several days earlier, our fighter planes made air strikes to neutralize the area for the coming invasion. On the 16th, the *Franklin*, which was firing on the invasion area, was hit on the deck edge by an enemy plane, but she continued on striking hits at Manila Bay.

As we neared Leyte, it was still under pre-invasion bombardment. A protective smoke screen settled over the landing area, and visibility was very poor. The underwater mine demolition crew had cleared the area, and I hoped none were missed. The surf was quite calm, and although the counter firing by the Japanese was ferocious, it did not seem quite as earth shattering as Saipan.

I watched the scene from the flying bridge, as we pulled into our anchorage area. The area was flat at the water's edge, giving rise to small sand dune crater areas. There at the beachhead a long line of LCIs, converted to rocket ships, were blasting their rockets onto the shoreline and into the rough terrain above.

Nothing was spared. Palm trees and shredded fronds spewed into the air; trees were sheared off as though a giant mowing machine had passed through. Mud and bushes were reduced to a mulched mass that splattered everything in sight. I doubted that even the pesky land crabs had survived the barrage of rockets. I thought of the landing about to take place, and the troops about to land. At least there would not be any snipers or machine gun nests on the beach. The LCIs finished their job and pushed on. Now our show was ready to start. To our relief the overhead firing had quieted down some, but we could hear the shattering booms of the battle engagements on both sides of the island. The pre-invasion bombardment had done a great job, and we moved the troops and supplies to shore in record time.

By midday, I noticed a commotion down the beach. The flagship cruiser *Nashville* was anchored out, and I noticed a contingent of officers had debarked, and were now wading in the water heading for shore. It certainly looked unusual. I heard someone say, "It's MacArthur!" There was no mistake. He had returned, and there he was striding in the surf. He had the president of the Philippines beside him, followed by his immediate staff of officers. I had a strong urge to rush over for a greeting, but the wounded needed help, for they were piling up on the beach for transport back to the ship, and there was still danger from Japanese torpedo planes.

We had only boarded a few casualties when a Japanese torpedo plane, seeming from out of nowhere, came from behind a small craggy hill behind the beach. The cruiser *Honolulu* was far up in the shallows, and the plane passed us up for the cruiser. I held my breath as the torpedo hit the cruiser and I saw the torpedo lodge in the fantail, with the explosive hanging over the side. Very slowly the explosive eased harmlessly into the water. This whole scene lasted a few minutes, but it seemed like a lifetime. (I learned afterward that the cruiser had already been torpedoed and was purposely in shallow water for repairs. The hits did not seriously damage her, and later she returned to Pearl for repairs.)

We had been working full speed all day, and were still cleaning up when the communications boat gave us a frantic signal for all the small crafts to drop everything and return to the transport immediately. H.P. and I looked around for our boat hook, who had not been any help all day, and now he had completely disappeared. We did not have time to play nursemaid; our orders were to leave, so we had to leave without him. (Later we discovered he left with the troops, joined up with the Army, got wounded and was finally sent back to the Navy.) We guessed he did not like the hard work with the amphibs; anyway, he did not come back to our crew.

The *Clay* pulled anchor as ordered, and led a formation of undamaged transports out of the Leyte Gulf and into the Philippine Sea.

Our operation that day, in spite of the heavy smoke, debris and gunfire, was so swift the Japanese reported the *Clay* transport sunk, for they felt no ship could unload and leave the gulf so fast. Leyte was a crucial objective, and the Japanese threw everything they had at us from both sides of the island, but our amphibians, ground forces, battleships, cruisers and destroyers gave them hell, and they turned and headed for their home base. For some reason or other a small jeep carrier and a destroyer failed to leave the gulf area, and a small part of the Japanese fleet broke through the beachhead area and sent them to the bottom.

"Sat. Oct. 21, 1944 Nine months since I last saw Ann."

The fighting moved inland and the beach area started to come to life. Natives who had survived the invasion paddled out to the ship in their little bumboats loaded with stalks of the small, sweet bananas to trade. We did not have much to trade so we threw some of our clothing over the side, and then lowered a rope for the bananas. Our clothing was in bad shape after the stress of the invasions, and one little native shook his fist and shouted something at us, holding up a sorry looking pair of dungarees with the crotch completely torn out … so much for native trade.

"Tues. Oct. 24, 1944 Left Leyte today for Hollandia, Dutch New Guinea."

"Thur. Oct. 26, 1944 Nine months since I left the States."

"Sun. Oct. 29, 1944 Arrived Hollandia, Dutch New Guinea."

The invasion of Hollandia six months earlier had been carefully planned. The Japanese had over 300 aircraft on the airfields about the island, and our air assaults almost completely wiped them out. These air assaults were a deciding factor for future landings. The newly designed amphibious craft was not yet in use, and each attack group had LSDs, which brought tanks to the target. Troops, stretcher-bearers, and supplies had to file down narrow ramps into the water, making the landing slow and treacherous. Unfortunately, after they possessed the airstrips, the heavy bombers could not use the airfield.

We dropped anchor outside the harbor, and the island was a beehive of activity. There were several large floating dry docks in the process of making small repairs on damaged boats. Engine parts, damaged boats, and supplies were in disarray in their hurry to get boats back into action again.

As soon as our boat was in the water, H.P. and I took off for the short mail run into the harbor. We were like kids out of school; the salt wind in our faces, and power behind the wheel—we felt half human again. As we carefully maneuvered through the harbor congestion, we heard a call of greeting and a loud whistle from the deck of a huge, floating dry dock. There, about forty feet above us, was Captain Abdill, our former captain. He was also from Alexandria, Virginia. He had noticed our boat number APA-39-17, his former command ship number.

Author's note: We did not realize this would be the last time we would see the captain. He had been assigned flagship officer aboard the light cruiser *Nashville*. Fifteen days later, on December 13, the light cruiser *Nashville*, escorting transports from Leyte to Mindoro, approached Leyte Gulf. The Japanese ,who had revived their air power with kamikaze tactics, sneaked in low, and crashed on the *Nashville* stern, port side, causing fire to break out. One hundred thirty-three officers and men were killed, including Admiral Struble and Captain E. W. Abdill.

H.P. and I thought the captain wanted to talk, so we circled the boat around to continue the conversation, and he seemed genuinely pleased to see us. The ship and crew were anxious for the mail and supplies, so we moved on to the dock. And what to our wondering eyes did we see? A small gathering of servicemen on the dock, and right in their midst girls … girls from the Women's Auxiliary Corp. The push and shove was on as all hands wanted to see. One sailor (there is one in every crowd) in a spirited conversation with one of the girls, suggested a swap of shirts. I can still hear the whistles and catcalls as she called his bluff. Before we could blink an eye, she peeled her shirt off for the exchange. I had never seen a khaki army bra before, not many bras at all in fact. We all had something to laugh and write home about (maybe not). I'll bet the sailor still has that shirt.

"Thu. Nov. 2, 1944 Left Hollandia this morning for Morotai."

Morotai had been secured around the 15th of September, virtually unopposed, and the Army Engineers and Royal Australian Air Force construction squadron moved in. The Japanese still had a large garrison and eight airfields nearby on the big island of Halmahera. Morotai was protected, but getting there left us wide open to attacks from enemy bombers.

"Sun. Nov. 5, 1944 Arrived Morotai, Netherland East Indies."

Japanese planes from the big island of Halmahera were watching our convoy and we had constant battle station duty night and day. We were relieved when we reached the protected area of Morotai. The air base was to be relocated, and we were to transport the ground crew and supplies to Leyte.

I was able to pick up some souvenir Dutch money with "Netherlands-Indies" printed on the front and a picture of

Netherlands Queen Wilhelmina on the back; something more for my sea bag cache.

"Wed. Nov. 8, 1944 Saw Frank today."

I saw the USS *Frederic Funston* in the docking area, and I knew Frankie would be ashore. I had not seen him for a long time, and we had a chance to talk. He was concerned about his wife, Esther, and the baby. He hoped she would be better this time and was as anxious to get this war over with and get home as I was.

The persistent Japanese planes kept us at our general quarters every night. On the third evening, we were watching a movie by the protected superstructure on deck, when the bosun piped lights out and GQ on the double. Japanese planes bugged our anchorage, sending us scurrying. The big army searchlights lit up the sky with their powerful beams, and they opened up their Long Toms in a mighty crescendo of booming gunfire. It was enough to wake the dead, and the planes turned with a flash of tail and returned to their base. The next night they were right back again.

For five nights we endured their gunfire, and with their air raids they dropped a phosphorus bomb, which spread an eerie light, and the noise trauma from the Long Toms kept our ears ringing for days.

What a relief to be finished loading our supplies and getting the Air Base ground crew aboard. The ground crew had been on Morotai for several months and had adopted birds and monkeys for pets. Before we pulled anchor a patrol boat came along side and announced that all pets, parrots and monkeys must be left with the patrol boat. The birds were beautiful, and they hated to part with their pets. We watched from the deck and gasped in horror and amazement as one of the ground crew took his pet monkey down the gangway to the water, and drowned the little animal right before our eyes. We never knew his reasoning, but to us it was senseless cruelty.

"Fri. Nov. 10, 1944 Left Morotai today, bound for Leyte."

Our nerves and muscles had been strained to the limit with the loading and the GQ alerts. We now had a little time to eat, but I don't know how the cooks managed. They had GQ also and still had the chow ready. I had lost over 15 pounds and I looked like a brown string bean; many days it was just beans and corn bread. I missed the fresh milk most of all. We had taken on tubs of butter from New Zealand, and it was white like mutton fat; tasted like it too. By now we were used to weevils in the bread; in this warm climate they appeared like magic. With the troops aboard, the cooks worked around the clock, and we all agreed that the "beef" they served was really kangaroo, but since it was hot the troops did not complain.

My tooth had been bothering me since the last invasion and finally I had a chance to see the dentist. He treated the abscessed tooth, but it left a sensitive lump on my gum that failed to disappear.

There were a few side benefits being in the amphibious group. Whenever we took on supplies, some of the crates accidentally came apart, and according to the unwritten law of survival, some large cans—no name and no label—found their way to the secret compartment of our landing craft.

Some nights, when we had not been on board for chow, we would gather near our boats when the smoking lamp was out, and open up our surprise prize. One night it was fruit cocktail, and with a spoon from the mess hall we all took turns gulping down that sweet nectar from the gods. The best windfall ever happened on Wooten's boat. A crate of eggs, broken and misplaced, found its way to Wooten's secret compartment. Fresh eggs ... that caused some excitement, especially since a can of bacon had been stored in my boat, just waiting. The bosun had a hot plate in the radio shack, and with a generous portion of our loot for pay, he rented it out. Next stop ... the bakeshop. They hadn't seen eggs lately either. More eggs and bacon were exchanged for a loaf of bread and an onion. Now we were all set, waiting for lights out.

It was quiet and as dark as the inside of a boot. We devoured those egg sandwiches like we had never seen an egg before. (It had been so long we could not remember.) We were afraid that the delicious smell would wake up the whole ship, but there was no one to know except the night watch, and he probably thought that delicious smell was coming from the officer's quarters. We felt a little guilty, but not much. It's called survival.

"Mon. Nov. 13, 1944 Attacked this afternoon by Japanese torpedo bombs. Plane shot down."

Our convoy was two days out of Morotai, when the bosun piped battle stations. We had two screens of destroyers out, and two screens of destroyers guarding our perimeters. The Japanese torpedo bombers had spotted our convoy, and immediately the destroyers circled and fired their guns like demons. In just a few minutes they had shot down seven or eight planes. In the midst of all the melee, one bomber slipped through the screen. He was flying very low, too low to be shot down; he circled and swooped between the transports headed right for our ship. We watched dumbfounded as he zoomed past our starboard bow, scarcely twenty feet above the water, and we braced for the torpedo to be released. He turned abruptly for what he thought was bigger game, a light cruiser at the end of the convoy. It was not a cruiser, but an LSD mounted with 5 inch guns fore and aft, and so agile it swerved sharply to starboard as the torpedo plane fired. We watched the incredible scene as the torpedo bounced once, twice, three times, to land harmlessly in the water. With the speed of a viper, the LSD turned and fired, and the bomber exploded and crashed. I said a little prayer for those gunners; another close call!

"Tues. Nov. 14, 1944 Arrived in Leyte this morning, unloaded cargo, left Leyte this afternoon for Manus."

Manus, the largest island of the Admiralties, had been in American hands for seven months. This area was extremely important, because we were now in control of the deep, landlocked harbor fifteen miles long and four miles wide. This was now a very active staging point, and the harbor was seeded with combat ships, patrol boats, amphibious craft, mine sweepers, hydrographic ships, and various kinds of service boats; all service ready and bobbing at anchor as far as the eye could see

"MON. NOV. 20, 1944 ARRIVED MANUS THIS MORNING. TEN MONTHS SINCE I LAST SAW ANN."

"TUES. NOV. 21, 1944 SAW MOVIE *CAREER GIRL*, RECEIVED CHRISTMAS PACKAGE FROM THE FOLKS. TEN MONTHS SINCE I LAST SAW ANN."

"SAT. NOV. 25, 1944 SAW MOVIE *SUMMER STORM* TONIGHT."

"SUN. NOV 26, 1944 10 MONTHS SINCE I LEFT THE STATES."

"MON. NOV. 27, 1944 LEFT MANUS TODAY FOR NEW BRITAIN."

"TUES. NOV. 28, 1944 ARRIVED CAPE GLOUCESTER, NEW BRITAIN, TODAY."

We dropped anchor at Borgen Bay to get our boats and gear in preparation for the big invasion of Luzon at Lingayen Gulf. We had a mail call, and I got a letter from Ann dated September 28, 1944, our anniversary. It took a month to get here.

From: Mrs. William C. Stein, R#4, Box 447, Alexandria, Va.

To: William C. Stein MOMM2/c Amphibious Div. L, USS Clay c/o Fleet Post Office, San Francisco, Calif.

September 28, 1944

Dear Bill,

Two years ago this time remember what we were doing? Getting married, just in case you forgot.

Darling, they were happy hours, but God had other plans for us. It was not to be that we would stay together, and, darling, I had a

happy anniversary considering you were absent. At least we have everything to look forward to, and we love each other. So many married couples just are sorry they got married. Gee, honey, two years is a long time, but it seems like our love just keeps growing stronger. Did you ever think what a queer thing love is? We just did not go out and look for it, it came right to us, and we were so young, too. That is one thing we can thank God for. Remember the little prayer we said on our wedding night? I will say it tonight and hope you are doing the same.

On Calvin's trip home from Fort Benning last weekend, he said to me, "I would not mind going to war, if I had someone to fight for, waiting for me to come home to." He talked quite a while and said being away he could see I was growing nicer every day, and said he sure wished he had as much to come home to as Bill has. Darling, he has been a dear brother to me, and I try to do everything I can for him. When he kissed me good-bye he almost cried; I did a little. This is mostly an anniversary love letter but I will tell you, we had a party at my house tonight. Bea and Ida came to dinner, and we gave Bea her birthday gifts. We had a cake for both of us, and had a fine time. I received six anniversary cards. Mrs. Taylor called and said she missed her star border. Happy anniversary, darling, Remember I love you, and I always will. I will wait for you, don't forget it.

All my love always,

Your Ann

P.S. I wore my blue wedding suit today. Hope you like the cartoon.

The cartoon was a cute girl wearing men's boxer shorts in the department store saying, "I may look silly, but the department manager said he wanted me in men's underwear today."

Received another letter from Ann dated Nov. 14, 1944:

Tues. 10:45 P.M.

Dear Bill,

Bea and I went to the show Till We Meet Again. *It was another war picture. We saw a dancing horse on stage and enjoyed it very much. Bea got a transfer to my office now, and it seems so nice to have her around. Ida is going home to Rhode Island and has only a few weeks left in Washington. I am taking annual leave tomorrow. I will go shopping for a coat, shoes and a few gifts. We still have not heard from Calvin; I suppose he will be shipping out soon. I'm lonely for you, honey, and I sure would like to lean close to you and say, "Gimme a kiss." Good night for now, honey, I love you. XXXXX*

"Sun. Dec. 3, 1944 My leave at home started one year ago today."

The mailroom fixed us up with a real nice V-mail Christmas card. It had a lighted candle, and underneath "Seasons Greetings from the USS *CLAY*." It was nice to have something special to send to the folks and Aunt Mabel.

"Thu. Dec. 7, 1944 Received mail and packages today."

Pearl Harbor anniversary day … a day for retaliation!

"Sat. Dec. 9, 1944 Left New Britain today for Manus, Admiralty Islands."

"Tues. Dec. 12, 1944 Amphibs sent ashore."

Our amphibious division was told to take two or three boats and go ashore. The ship had to go out to sea and test the engines. I don't know if our boats were in the way or if they wanted to get us off the deck; probably both. We took off for shore and considered it a free day, like a beach party. I was concerned about where we were going to eat, and we were told, "Just catch the mess hall at one of the anchored destroyers." We all decided a beach party without beer would be no party at all, so we asked the officer if he could buy some for us. He bought us a case, and we attempted to drink as many as we could: big mistake, lunchtime passed by. We were all pretty sloshed by this time and I had hunger pangs. We picked the nearest destroyer, and since it had bumpers around the sides, we did no damage as our double vision tried to bring our boats to the gangway. The officer of the deck smiled and looked away, and I gave a sigh of relief. I really hoped he was thinking, *Those amphibs have a hell of a job and they need a day to relax.* We explained our situation, and the officer called for an escort who led, I should say helped, us to the mess hall. The dinner was fit for a king! What a meal; real chopped beef, mashed potatoes and green peas. I thought I had died and gone to heaven. Not that our cooks weren't good. In all fairness they had an army to feed, and that's a bit different than just a ship's crew. After that glorious meal, we sobered up immensely, enough to thank the OD for his patience and the great meal. Our exit was much more professional than our entrance.

Back in the boats, we still had half a case of beer to get rid of and we were due back to the ship. We drank a few more ourselves, and as we passed the destroyers, the crews were laughing and waving so we used our pitching arms and threw the remaining cans of beer into welcoming hands, causing quite a commotion, to say the least.

"Fri. Dec. 15, 1944 Saw the movie *Story of Dr. Wassell* tonight."

The staging area was bustling with activity, and we were working to adjust cargo. There seemed to be no end to loading and unloading supplies and troops.

"Sat. Dec. 16, 1944 Left Manus today."

"Mon. Dec. 18, 1944 My leave at home ended one year ago today."

"Wed. Dec. 20, 1944 Eleven months since I last saw Ann, seems like so long."

"Thu. Dec. 21, 1944 Arrived back in Manus today."

We were back in the staging area, and had more supplies to move. We took on some injured, and the sick bay was filled again. We had mail call and I received a letter from Ann, and a picture. She looked a little different and sad with her long hair done up in French braids. I also received a Christmas card from Aunt Mabel.

"Fri. Dec. 22, 1944 Saw movie *Barberry Coast Gent* tonight."

"Sat. Dec. 23, 1944 Saw movie *Star Spangled Rhythm* tonight."

"Sun. Dec. 24, 1944 Received Ann's Christmas card tonight. I feel empty this Christmas Eve because my heart is at home."

The card from Ann contained a Christmas bond certificate. It had Disney characters in color around the edge. "From the United States Treasury, War Finance Committee."

"This is to certify that William Charles Stein MOMM 2/c is the owner of a War Bond, thereby becoming an investor in this country's fight for human liberty and a contributor in a world struggle to make life free and forever peaceful for all men. This bond presented by Mrs. William Charles Stein attested this 25-day of December 1944."

Ann sent me a Christmas card also, and it really made me homesick.

To my husband:
You mean the world and all to me, I've told you so before.
But Christmas is the perfect time to tell you so once more.
And Christmas is the time to wish the best things life can hold.
For you the one I love so much, as the days and weeks unfold.
All my love, Ann

"MON. DEC. 25, 1944 CHRISTMAS ON MANUS."

Christmas on Manus. I could hardly take a breath it was so humid and hot. Absolutely no sign of snow. The bosun piped, "Now hear this, Merry Christmas. All hands top side. Santa Claus is coming aboard the USS *Clay*."

Sure enough, Santa was there standing in the captain's boat on deck. Lt. Commander Archie Simonstad gave him a big welcome. The crew had hooked up a bullhorn to call out the names of the crew; everyone received a gift, and I was happy to receive a nice brown leather DOP kit, which I needed.

Christmas in Manus was nothing to write home about, but I was still alive, and the pain I could live with. The cookies from home did not last long, and I worried about how many more hazardous days would pass until Tokyo was in our hands.

"TUES. DEC. 26, 1944 ELEVEN MONTHS SINCE I WAS LAST IN THE STATES."

"WED. DEC. 27, 1944 LAE, NEW GUINEA, MANEUVERS AND REHEARSALS FOR LUZON INVASION."

The only thing different about rehearsals was the troops. For us it was the same old routine. However, we had seen for a fact that our landing routines had saved many lives, if only for the fact of speed. We kept our engines and equipment in top shape. We were constantly oiling, greasing, tearing down and putting together, and we learned to do it in the dark. The troops also learned that the Navy did more than just sail the seas, and that the amphibs were going to do their best to get them safely to their destination on shore.

"SUN. DEC. 31, 1944 BURIAL AT SEA FOR FOUR SOLDIERS FROM OUR SICK BAY WE WERE TRANSPORTING."

As soon as we hit open water, we were told to prepare for another burial at sea. Four soldiers from our sick bay died of wounds from the last invasion. It was a very sad and moving service, and now we were hurrying to the site of another invasion. Our transport was so loaded with troops and supplies the decks were a hazard. The passage to Luzon was treacherous to say the least, for Japanese-held islands were all along the way. We were sailing in very dangerous waters, and the radio room informed us that the Japanese were now staging suicide attacks by crashing directly on the ships. This was a real nail biter, and we stayed at battle stations around the clock.

"Mon. Jan. 8, 1945 Saw suicide bomber at battle station."

A suicide bomber headed directly at us today. There was no doubt in my mind that our luck had run out, and there was no time for a survival plan either; I could only stare at the pilot as his face came into view. With just a few seconds left until oblivion, the pilot spotted a carrier and swerved to bag larger game. We all watched from the deck as the scene played before our eyes. The Japanese pilot, heading for certain death, crashed on the carrier deck, and all hands rushed to douse the fire and shove the blazing bomber over the side and into the water. I couldn't believe that we had lucked out again, and I am really getting good at this prayer thing.

"Tues. Jan. 9, 1945 S-Day for Luzon."

Unlike the invasion of Leyte, the three-day pre-invasion bombardment was defended ferociously by the Japanese. They were using a different tactic; the kamikaze bomber. The bay was a sea of ships, minesweepers, destroyers, escort carriers, demolition units, gunboats, battleships and various types of amphibious craft. The time was set and we went ashore with the worst bombardment that we had ever seen. Our ship's guns were firing over our heads, and the kamikazes were crashing on any ship they could find. Their fuel and bombs caused raging infernos, and flaming gasoline seared the lungs and limbs of our officers and men. It was a bold and daring landing and combat ships were sending explosives over our heads. The gunners on our transport were in a frenzy trying to repel the suicide bombers, while we rushed to get the troops down the cargo nets and the supplies safely to shore. The fallout was pelting us from all sides as we kept an eye out and an ear to communications to keep from getting blown up by our own fire.

It would soon be daylight and we had just started another cargo run when a Japanese torpedo boat swooped in and fired on a transport near us. It was still dark and army troops were sleeping in their bunks waiting for their turn to invade. The torpedo blew a huge hole in the side of the transport and as the water rushed in, the men who were sleeping jetted out the open space. Oil and fire covered their bodies. At that time our worst fear was that the bomber would return to finish the job, but we scooped them up with our ramp and headed for shore. They were in shock, shivering and shaking. Oil was everywhere, even in their hair and eyes. We cleaned them off with our shirts and sand, and then took a chance and built a fire to calm them and warm them up. We hoped the Japanese wouldn't bother with such a small target.

The worst part was the screams of the burn victims, and to add to our troubles the cruiser *Boise* was attacked. We heard MacArthur was aboard for a conference, and to add to our misery, the surf, which was deceptively smooth, contained huge ground swells. Landing craft had a terrible time, and even an LST was beached on its side. It seemed the debarking would never end. So much time was lost just trying to avoid death. We were interrupted from our regular tasks for another casualty recovery. A destroyer escort had taken a direct hit and all crafts in the immediate area were directed to rescue and transport. The first bodies we reached had been blown clear of the wreckage. Some were charred instantly by the tremendous heat from the fuel. The bodies, soaked and burned, were a dead weight, and we had all we could do to lift them out of the water without falling into the blazing inferno ourselves. The scent of burning flesh is like no other, and it leaves an acrid, corrosive film in the lining of your nose and throat that lasts for days. How much stress can the human body stand? Charred and blackened bodies with arms raised, tying to shield their faces. Faces burned beyond recognition with teeth bared in a grimace of death. We opened up those powerful motors, and with horror all around us, delivered more dead and maimed to the hospital ship.

In spite of our loading interruptions, we had retained our record for one day unloading, and by sundown our job was completed … almost. I still had a watch to stand. The Japanese were attempting to swim to the transports disguised under a crate, straw hat, box or driftwood, and attach bombs to the sides of the ships. On our watch we paced the area, firing our 45 automatics at anything and everything floating in the water. I don't know if we ever hit any enemy, but we blasted away, and it helped wear off some of the day's frustration and pain. I was glad when we pulled anchor for Leyte to pick up more troops to bring back to Luzon. We had endured another three days of complete hell.

"Sat. Jan. 13, 1945 Back to Luzon."

After debarking troops and supplies, a few of us from our amphibious division were given orders to take our crafts to the beaching area. Several boats and amphibs were sent from other transports, and joined us there. The Army needed us to instruct their men on how to operate and maintain small boats for an upriver penetration. The boats would bring more supplies and material for an all out advance on Manila.

The army guys were great, and willing to take orders from sailors! They knew we were specially trained, and they were anxious to learn. The beach at Lingayen was splattered with wrecked boats of all kinds, and the countryside was in sorry shape. A few huts were still partially standing, and the natives who had weathered the invasion were now cautiously appearing. Soon a small group had gathered and we were amazed at the welcome they gave us. Others appeared laughing and offering those small sweet bananas. We did not have much in exchange. The Army had a few blankets, K rations, toothpaste, and candy. I had a small stash in my secret compartment on my boat … a can of salmon, and two of baked beans. Soon there were many eager hands reaching for food. The women were in bad shape, their clothing ragged and the children barely dressed.

The OP in our party had a small camera, and he took pictures of our "beach party" with Pig, Stinky, myself and the native girls, clutching the few things we gave them. The OP sent me the pictures later, and I was thankful to him, at least it proved I was there … as if I needed proof. At the edge of the small group, I noticed a man with a woman who was very pregnant; her dress barely covered her distended body. I remembered my soft, white Navy blanket in my boat. When she saw me with it in my hands her face lit up in a toothy smile. I handed the blanket to the man, thinking he was her husband. To my amazement, he snatched it and ran. I will never forget the look on her face, as her eyes filled with tears. I was so angry with the little thief, I pulled out my 45 automatic and shot several times over his head, but he ran like a bat out of hell without even looking around. I had nothing more to give her; I had even given away my extra pair of work dungarees earlier that day.

The natives had piles of Japanese money in exchange for anything we could give them. The money was worthless now, but I wanted some to store in my sea bag. The words *Japanese Government* were printed on the top and the word *Peso* or *Centavo* printed over the front with numbers on each corner. Before the invasion of Leyte, we had been issued currency to be used when we got ashore. "Philippines" was printed on the front, with a picture of Mabin, "Victory Series #66, payable to the bearer on demand in silver pesos or in legal tender." A big blue seal was printed with "Commonwealth of the Philippines, United States of America." "VICTORY" was stamped on the backside. We gave the natives a few of our bills, but they had no place to spend them.

We ate at the army mess and slept in tents with the sides rolled up, suffering through the mosquito attacks and the land crab raids, but they were a great group of guys, and I guess they learned enough to get them to Manila and back, and we were glad to be ferried back to the *Clay*.

"Sat. Jan. 20, 1945 Back to Leyte, shifting supplies and embarking the 1st Calvary Troops for replacement landings on Luzon."

I was surprised to receive a letter from Ann's nephew, Larry.

December 31, 1944

Dear Uncle Bill:

Ann wandet me to rite you a letter. How are you feeling? Will you get me a souvenir please? There is snow on the grond for Xmas. Got one Heilocopter and a pair of slippers and some games. Ann gave me a wool shirt.

I slept with Ann last nite, don't you wish you were here. Get a Jap for me and get what he has on him and brang it home to Ann for me.

Larry

"Wed. Jan. 24, 1945 Moonlight torpedo attack."

The Japanese were not satisfied to torture us all day with their suicide attacks; they were using the moonlight to scare us to death. There was no sleep, for battle stations were manned constantly. To make matters worse, they came back late at night. One attacked our transport just when we thought they had surely gone home to bed. Everything had been quiet at my battle station when I heard that dreaded drone of a bomber. There was no mistaking it. He slipped between our transport and the one behind. I hoped the gunners had not fallen asleep from exhaustion. When I saw the flash of flame, and heard the crash and splash I knew our gunners had another plane to their credit, but how many more would come tomorrow?

"Fri. Jan. 26, 1945 Leyte, P.I. Received letter from Bill Allen."

We boarded on troops from the 1st Calvary Division, to take them to Lingayen. The *Clay* was again bulging at the sides, but we got a mail call, and I had a long letter from Bill.

From: T/4 William S. Allen 32264383, 71 AAA Opr. Dct. APO 464, c/o PM New York, New York

To: William C. Stein MOMM 2/c, USS Clay, L Div. Amphibious, c/o Fleet P.O., San Francisco, Calif.

Northern Italy, January 8, 1945.

Dear Bill,

I am sending Dave's address. 14117927, Co. c Infantry, APO 15591, C/o Postmaster, New York, N. Y.

Well here it is another year starting; I wonder where it will end. Still we are at war and a hell of a long way from getting back to Wenonah. So you were in the Leyte invasion, I thought that you were. I'd like to hear your personal account or isn't that permissible? I have written you several letters recently, and a Christmas card. Perhaps, though by now you have received them. I sure hope so, for I know how much mail means.

So you are going to settle with me over my writing your wife eh!!! Come on ahead. I dare you. In fact I double dare you for I'd sure like to have another reunion like we had in Oran. That was really swell. I'll never forget how you looked that first afternoon you were on watch on a landing craft down over the side of the ship. I came over to the rail and leaned over and yelled, "Hey, Bill." You looked up and couldn't seem to believe your eyes, then you seemed to blink, then you hailed me in return. Our mouths didn't stop for about five hours. I believe it was until I had to leave.

Remember that walk on that Sunday afternoon in the park? High overlooking Oran Harbor, and how we looked at the women!! You got home after that, but poor me; I'm still sweating out for a furlough.

Ann sure has been swell to me and faithful. I think that she feels that I am the "Second Husband." Hope you aren't jealous!

I got three different packages from Ann this Christmas. I feel almost overawed, for I know how difficult it is to get these luxuries back home. I do, however, really think she enjoys doing things like that for us.

Did I tell you Aunt Mabel sent me a package? I got, all told, about

18 or 20 packages.

How did you fare on the Christmas gift side this year? I hope your mail was not held up much. Tell me all about what you did Christmas day. I worked so you see I did very little celebrating or service going. I went to service the previous Sunday and really enjoyed singing carols; reminded me of Ann, and the choir at church.

Dave is in France. I got a card at Christmas saying that he is a "Doughboy," so I guess that he is in the infantry. Good luck to him! Boy, if he is in the infantry, he sure needs it.

My Italian flame has burned down to perhaps very low or completely out, for I am unable to see her now, and I probably will never again have the opportunity to go back.

Kay is fast becoming a faithful writer. I told you about her in my last letter. She signs her letter "Love, Kay" and puts other little inferences of "amour" besides having sent three (3) photos of herself.

Well, all I can wish you in the way of good luck and cheer and hope and safety, Bill, is yours.

Your Pal, Bill A.

"Sat. Jan. 27, 1945 Returned to Lingayen, and unloaded in one single day, and took on wounded for transport."

We unloaded supplies and a part of the 1st Calvary Division with minimum difficulty. Boarding the casualties was a little more difficult. Most were stretcher cases, but we knew they would get good hospital care in Guadalcanal.

"Mon. Feb. 12, 1945 Guadalcanal; debarked the wounded."

The wounded in stretchers had been spread all about the ship. We were glad they were to get hospital care, for our sick bay had limited facilities. It was off with the wounded, and on with the 3rd Battalion of the 29th Regiment, 6th Marine Division. Of course this meant more training maneuvers and practice with the division, to master the cargo nets and learning to debark in all manner of surf, over and over again.

There was tension in the air, for we could tell we were assembling for something big. The word was out to have every craft in readiness. Our forces were convening for a massive assault. I was sure the next step would be Okinawa.

"Wed. Feb. 14, 1945 Tulagi; received mail from Mother and Dad."

I received a valentine and a birthday card from Mother and Dad. The valentine had two red satin hearts on the front and printed, "With Special Thoughts of You." On the birthday card Mother wrote that there were three packages on the way. The picture on the front really made me homesick; it was a picture of a server with a phone on top, just like the one at home.

"Thu. Feb. 15, 1945 Tulagi; received two letters from Ann dated Jan. 27, and Feb. 2."

Ann's valentine was covered with hearts and XXXXXXX's. The writing said, "A Valentine for the Mr. from the Mrs. Loads of Love and Lots of Kisses." Another comic valentine said, "Guess who? And you better guess the right one, darn it." She enclosed a little note.

1/27/45

Bill,

Well, honey, here goes another holiday with you far away. It is cold here tonight. George is better, and we finally heard from Cal. He is pretty good. I feel lonely tonight and so disgusted at work. We have so much to do, and I scarcely get home when it's time to go back to work again. I sure wish you were here, I could tell them all to go to the devil and quit. Oh well, I'm just blue and there will be a day. Until then I'll go on working and saving. Good night, honey.

I love you, Ann

"Tues. Mar. 6, 1945 Tulagi. Received letter from Ann dated 2/26/1945."

The mail is coming through in a haphazard manner. The airmail letter cost 6 cents and the blue stamp had a Victory Eagle with "Win the War" across its chest. This letter was dated before I got the last one in February.

February 26, 1945

Dear Bill,

Tonight I was in a partial heaven. I received 3 letters from you tonight. They were so cheerful, I laughed out loud in the one where you were telling me about the arm of Evelyn's couch that we broke and Townie's kitchen sink, and talked about me taking advantage of you. You poor boy, just you wait till you come home this time. I'll take advantage of you all right.

Glad to hear you could play a little ball, of course you did not have me rooting for you. When you come home I hope you won't want to play softball rather than—

Yes, I've been working late, but I will take a couple of days off soon. Also 1&1/2 days when I go up home on the 25 of March. I will get Dad a birthday gift and send Aunt Lilly a card also; also Easter gifts for Aunt Mabel and Mother. Have you any suggestions for Dad's gift?

I did not know that you were on Manus Island. It will help me with your scrapbook. I have a lot of nice pictures. I have sent a few snapshots; the big pictures are not ready yet. They make me so angry; it has been three weeks now. Be patient, honey.

So you are going to show me just how much you love me when you get home, eh? Well, that's just what I'm waiting for. Come ahead, honey.

We just listened to Sherlock Homes and are now listening to Lux Radio. Cary Grant is in it. I saw the picture, but don't remember the name. It is raining tonight. I sent Cal some food, he said he doesn't get much but K rations. It has been so bitter cold in Germany where he is that his feet have been frost bitten, and he needs socks. I hope he gets them soon. A big lipstick kiss for you, honey, I love you, dear.

Ann

"WED. MAR. 21, 1945 ULITHE, CAROLINE ISLANDS."

At mail call I received an Easter card from Ann. It had a cute little bunny on the front with big tears on the cheeks; inside a cute little poem.

The flowers are bloomin', the bells are ringin'.
The sun's a shinin', the birds are singin'.
Things seem as usual, exceptin' I'm blue.
Can't think of nuthin', exceptin' just you.

Darling, this has been a busy day for your little Rooney. Went to church first thing. Honey, the weather is so balmy, and it seems like spring is around the corner. You know how that feels. This afternoon I washed and ironed my slips and blouses. I wear my black, orchid and blue suits to work mostly. I'm saving my best dresses for you. I have a black crepe dress with black lace neck and a black crepe dress with fuchsia trim, and my pink wool. I want to be all dressed up when you come home. I have all my household articles except cooking utensils and good dishes, but I have enough to start with.

Mother called me tonight. It was good to hear her voice, and it just cheered me up so I told her I would be up Palm Sunday.

Gee, work again tomorrow. It will be swell when I can get up and get your breakfast and stay home to take care of little "Bill." It will be fun, won't it, honey? So keep safe. I love you, dear, all my kisses,

Ann

P.S. I'm sending you a piece of material from my dress. A

"THU. MAR. 22, 1945 WROTE LETTER TO ANN TODAY."

March 22, 1945—USS Clay

Dear Annie:

Last night I received your Easter card and two letters; also a letter from Mom and Dad. The card was cute, honey. Thanks a lot. I wish I could send you a nice one the way I used to do. Just wishing you a Happy Easter is about all I can do for now.

I'm glad you got the pictures I sent OK. I thought maybe you would get a kick out of them. Don't worry about those pictures of yourself; if you can't get them that's not your fault. I know those things are pretty hard to get now.

You mentioned in one of your letters you would like a certain china set, so if that is what you have your heart set on, then that's what it will be. Let me know how much you will need and I'll send whatever you say as soon as I can.

Dad wrote that he was going to get glasses some time soon; gosh, I won't hardly know you people when I come home. I see by the church bulletin that a lot of the boys are still sweating it out in the States. I even read where one poor fellow was stationed 225 miles from his wife. She just couldn't find a place nearer than that. The worst part of it though, he only gets to see her every other weekend. Can you imagine the gall of anybody complaining about something like that? He's the kind I would like to see shoved out here on one of these beautiful Pacific atolls. Well, darling, I've just enough space to say I love you, and miss you so very much.

So long for now,
Bill

"Sun. Mar. 25, 1945 Ulithe."

Our training maneuvers with the Marines aboard left us weary and on edge. Water was in short supply again, and the troops tried to keep out of each other's way. It was not easy for they knew from past experience that we were in for a lot more trouble. It was now known that Okinawa would be our next objective.

Ships were again gathering from the many staging areas of the Pacific. Every day hundreds more arrived, extending our anchorage area. Japanese planes were spotted constantly, for there were several airfields on Okinawa, and also on nearby islands.

We awoke to the sound of pounding waves; a tremendous storm had covered the area, and waves washed the deck and bulkhead. I watched the appalling sight as hundreds of ships rose with the storm, and fell completely out of sight behind the crashing waves. I checked the security of our landing crafts, barely able to hold on. Our decks were a mess, the troops were sick and heaving anywhere they could. The damage to the galley left us without any hot food. Our transports were the most vulnerable, with their loaded decks. The battleships and aircraft carriers were solid in the water, but the smaller craft really took a beating.

By the next morning the waves were not as deadly, and we noticed a British battleship had arrived to join the great armada. Although the waves were still tremendous, we had orders to lower our crafts for taxi service. I was uneasy about the safety of our crafts, but some junior officers wanted to visit friends on ships anchored in the armada area. You can rest assured we gave them a ride, the ride of their lives, just short of a mishap in the briny deep. There has to be some justice in life.

"Easter Sunday April 1, 1945 D-Day, the battle for Okinawa."

Our convoy of gigantic proportions arrived at Okinawa before daylight. The seas were calm, but it soon became a violent morning. Smoke was so heavy you could cut it with a knife, for the invasion was preceded by five days of intensive bombardment as escort carriers, cruisers, battleships and gunboats covered the island with a solid blanket of gunfire.

The *Clay* dropped anchor about seven miles off shore, and we prepared for our part of the action. At first we were not able to see the jutting limestone bluffs that were honeycombed with caves and tunnels, but there behind the beach was a six-foot, concrete seawall. Our crafts and beach marker were color-coded and in place for our landing, and a soft shore breeze flapped our colored flags and parted the smoke for better visibility. Our waves were just a part of the powerful armada of landing crafts hurtling toward the smoke and fire on shore, and the waves of landing crafts extended as far as the eye could see along the coastal edge and also seaward. I'm sure that any Japanese observer from the garrisons on the cliff side must have been astounded by our perfectly orchestrated water ballet, in spite of the bombardment over head. Guns from the battleship *Tennessee* fired a battery of projectiles over our heads and into the cliffs. Japanese mortar batteries responded, causing great plumes of water around our boats. (Thankfully missing us.) LCI(G)s were firing with a continuous beating like Indian war drums, and my ears were ringing from the head-pounding noise of the rockets. Worst of all were the mass kamikaze attacks; there were more hits than misses, but we kept up our pace, and our unloading moved the troops up the beach. It seemed a little easy, but the Japanese were not about to give up the island, and by mid-morning transports filled the sea at the landing zone, and amtracs, tanks, troops and bulldozers were crawling and scraping up the hill. The mortar shells from the Japanese garrison on the bluff were still trying to get our range, but to our great relief, they just made giant splashes in the water. We were all too busy to observe the overall picture, but we saw many ships in flames and sinking. We lost count of the shore runs with ammo, rations and equipment, and it soon stacked up like checkers on a board. Debarking was accomplished by late afternoon, and the *Clay* pulled anchor to return to the staging area for more replacements and supplies.

After a perilous, frenzied four days and three nights of working with cranes and winches, loading, lifting, and working beyond endurance, the battered *Clay* and her crew pulled anchor for San Francisco on April 5, 1945, leaving the bloody battle for Okinawa, to transport more replacement troops.

Authors note: The Okinawa invasion was well planned and well manned, and Easter Sunday, April 1, 1945 became the last and most successful amphibious invasion of the war. The Americans fought on for over three months in the bloodiest slaughter of the entire Pacific War. 34 ships were sunk by the kamikazes, 763 carrier planes were lost, 4,907 sailors lost and 4,800 wounded. The Army lost 7,613 men with 31,800 wounded. In comparison, over 107,539 Japanese soldiers were killed, 27,769 were entombed in caves, and 10,755 were taken prisoner.

The Okinawa beachhead was a great struggle, and military history would record it as among the most intense and famous.

"Sun. April 8, 1945 Wrote a letter to Ann."

Sunday, April 8, 1945

Dear Ann,

Well, darling, this is my first letter to you for some time; I have been busy. I hope you have not been worrying about me too much. I'm still OK, just about the same as ever, I guess, missing you and hoping to see you soon. It seems like such a terrible time since I saw you last, but maybe it won't be too much longer.

I have not heard from you in quite a while either. I'm sorry the censors cut up my letters so much. I know it is hard for both of us to write and not reveal too much to the enemy, in case the mail gets in their hands. Heaven forbid. There is some chance we may get a few letters today.

The last pictures you sent were surely swell. Looks just like you. It is my favorite now; the colored one I mean.

Do you remember me writing to you about Joe? At the time I did not know about it, but he is on the Clay. *He said he remembers you from school. I just read the book* Leave Her to Heaven. *Be sure to read it if you get the chance.*

There has been no mail from Bill Allen for several months. Since you have heard from him, I suppose he is OK. I have not written anyone except you and the folks; been a little busy.

How is the watch coming along? It has been so many places with me that it is worth more in sentimental value than anything else.

So long for now, honey. Remember that I love you, won't you?

Love, Bill

"Mon. April 9, 1945 Saipan."

The *Clay* stopped briefly at Saipan. We made the mail run, and I had several letters, which I eagerly tore open, having not heard from home since March.

Mother and Dad sent an Easter card, which was mailed March 21, 1945; about 9 days en route. If they had known what I was going through Easter Day, it would have been far beyond their imagination, or anyone's, in fact. I also had a letter from Annie dated March 26.

March 26, 1945—9:45 P.M.

Darling,

I am adjusting myself after my trip up home. Sat. night Mother, Dad and I went to the Homestead, and had fried oysters. It reminded me of the times we ate there. Then we went to a movie and saw And Then Tomorrow*; it was a picture with Allan Ladd and Loretta Young. It was a good picture. Sunday was an eventful day, church and then to see your mother's brother, George. He is very bad off. Then we went to the store; Townie and Larry were there. I had on my new outfit and Townie kept watching me. I'd give a lot to know what he was thinking.*

He asked about you and everyone; he really looked bad. Evelyn used to keep his things looking nice. Then we took a chicken over to your uncle George, and saw Ralph. He was surprised to see me, and said I was looking nice, and asked about you. He is working at the New York shipyard now.

Then I went to see Dave's mom. She was in terrible shape, but so glad to see me. Of course she asked about you, and kept referring to you, Bill and Dave as the three musketeers. She showed me all of Dave's things, the Purple Heart and all. I just can't believe it, such a nice guy, and I guess he went in at the wrong time. It doesn't seem possible he is gone; we used to dance at the Band Box, and he really loved to swing.

Aunt Mabel came over, and she gave me gold earrings. Mother and Dad gave me the cutest pair of white gloves with little buttons on them. Also I gave Aunt Mabel the hanky and scarf you sent from Hawaii. She cried a little when she saw your writing on it.

Junior came over to see me about 9 P.M. He is a good kid and sort of clings to me now. He is confused, and feels so sad. I showed him the pictures of those poor natives. He and Donald got a big kick out of them. They are big boys now, and Junior actually seemed proud when I kissed him. I guess he is glad that someone really cares.

Your package arrived, and, darling, you are the most thoughtful husband in the world. Everything is grand. Will write more later.

Love, Ann XXXX

"FRI. APRIL 13 1945."

I felt almost guilty heading for Pearl while the fighting on the islands is still so extremely ferocious. The kamikazes were controlling everything, but how many more planes and pilots could they afford to lose? There's no doubt about it, when they crashed on deck they were either horribly burned or dead. The self-destroying acts of the Japanese were wearing us down; it took a strong, young crew to man battle stations day and night when sleep was a rare luxury.

Early in the morning on Friday the 13th, our bosun piped attention. "Attention, all hands! Now hear this. President Roosevelt is dead. Repeat, our Supreme Commander President Roosevelt is dead."

The ship was so quiet; you could hear the swish of the waves. This was a stunning blow. Who would command the action of this devastating war? Would Truman, our Vice President, be able to carry on?

"FRI. APRIL 20, 1945 PEARL HARBOR."

Thankfully our trip was fairly uneventful; the Japanese were out for bigger game, but now we had a lot of adjusting and work to do. We were in safe harbor and could finally sleep at night. On my first liberty to Honolulu, I met a part of our training crew from Fort Pierce ATB. They had been sent directly to the Pacific for the invasion of Tarawa. Still visibly in shock, they told how the wide coral reef had damaged their crafts and the tide was so low the troops had a long wade to shore under heavy fire. On that D-Day morning, November 20, 1943, more than a thousand marines and sailors bathed the sands with their blood, and many drowned with their full packs on. The reason the losses were so high was due to the fact that the amphibs had yet to receive the specially equipped command ships that were so critical to saving time and lives. Our landing craft were in bad shape, a few were missing, and I was just wondering how we were going to patch them up, when orders came through to hoist them off the ship for repair at the dry dock. The order happened so fast I was unable to remove my stash of canned goods in the secret compartment. I also bemoaned the loss of my thick Navy blanket that had rocked me to sleep on deck. I soon forgot my losses with the thought of San Francisco, and the only reason we would be glad to leave Hawaii. The night before we pulled anchor, I stood on the deck, high above the city. Everything seemed like a dream; the soft breeze laden with the scent of ginger blossoms, the people walking under the palm trees. It was so far removed from the horrible sound of the toys of war.

Allen, a member of the ship's company, was a printer/draftsman by trade. He was transferring off the *Clay* for they needed him elsewhere. He told us he would make a map of the *Clay's* ports of call and invasions for $5.00 each. (I had forgotten about the map, but several months later he sent a beautiful map in color to my home. It was 36 X 22 inches, with sketches of interesting happenings, and all ports of call in the Asiatic theater. Along with the beautiful map, he had included the *Clay* Odyssey, noting ports of call, invasions, and other interesting details. However, the map did not include the invasion of Tinian or Okinawa, or my European landings. These occurred when he was not on the ship. This map has a place of honor on my family room wall.) Thank you, Allen.

"May 10, 1945 San Francisco."

The Golden Gate Bridge was a sight for battle-sore, bloodshot eyes. We dropped anchor at Mare Island, and unloaded our ammunition and explosives. For once we could unload at an even pace and not be concerned about bombs bursting all around us, and our nerves were starting to calm down.

The sight of California looked like heaven to us as we hugged the coast northward. We passed Oakland, and eased into the Kaiser Shipyard at Richmond.

By this time I was fairly jumping out of my skin, but we still had a lot of work to do. Our ship went into dry dock for much-needed repairs, and they were going to add heavier armament. I wondered if there was enough armament in the world to protect us from the tenacious kamikazes.

"TUES. MAY 15, 1945 GIVEN 15 DAYS OF SHORE LEAVE."

Fifteen days of shore leave, and home sweet home. Seven days for travel and eight days of bliss. H.P., Wooten and I were riding high as we headed for Oakland. The lines at the telephones were twenty deep, but I finally got a line through to Ann and the folks.

We had lunch at a small restaurant, where there was a sign in the window. "Servicemen welcome home. All the free milk you can drink." And did we drink! Our train was not scheduled to leave until 7 P.M., so we purchased a few bottles of the hard stuff, and a bag of oranges.

The loading platform was a sea of servicemen and women. It was the largest jam imaginable, and we were lucky to get tickets. We walked through many cars before we found a place for four. We put our gear in the fourth seat hoping to save it for someone we knew. We settled in and started on our refreshments. I do remember dozing a little, and sucking on those sweet oranges. Soon we aroused to find the oranges were all gone, so we started drinking the bourbon straight from the bottle. Our minds were a little foggy about where we were, and I don't know who made the suggestion, but the idea was to walk through all the cars and look for Japs. It was a preposterous idea, but our bodies and minds were still in the battle zone. There was one very scary incident, as they told me later. I cornered a sailor, who had particularly slanted eyes, and had him down on the floor in a chokehold. At this time, as good luck would have it, my stomach rebelled with the unaccustomed alcohol, and was seriously considering an upheaval all over the passengers. I released my hold on the sailor's throat and Wooten dragged me into the head, just in time. I couldn't believe it; Stein with the cast iron stomach was going to throw up. I barely remembered them dragging me to my seat and from then on it was sweet violets.

A jolting train noise finally aroused me, and I was wide-awake. When it finally dawned on me where I was, my mind flashed to my wallet. We had been paid in Hawaii and I had $400 in $20 dollar bills with the words HAWAII printed across the back. I patted my pocket again … empty! What a fool I had been. Someone had rolled me but good, and all for a bottle of booze. I thought about Annie. She was not going to like this one bit. Feeling dejected, I looked around for H.P. and Wooten; fine pals they were to leave me alone.

I heard some noise down by the observation platform. There they were laughing and grinning at my thunderous expression. I'm glad the joke was on me, they had my wallet, and my loot was safe.

The train stopped at Reno, and we all staggered out to stretch our legs. We noticed a cute—the sight of any girl was cute—little girl on the platform sitting on her suitcase. Alas, she had no seat on the train, but lo, in her midst were three macho sailors, who grabbed her suitcase and hoisted her aboard. She could see there were no extra seats, but sea bags were reshuffled and lo and behold a seat for the little lady, right with us.

She was the only female, at least in our car, and we were stepping high as we escorted her to the dining car. It had been fourteen months since we were in the States, and close to a real live woman, and we were all a little bit giddy. At night we shoved the seats back, and made a cozy bed with our P jackets to keep us warm, and the competition was on for the closest cuddling.

We were all deflated when our little prize left our charming company in Chicago, and we piled our bags back on her vacated seat. As new passengers boarded, we thought our luck for another female companion had run out. One of the uniforms passing by was a girl, a wave ensign, no less. A red warning flag flashed through my mind, but an early swig of bourbon quelled the thought. Better the brig than a trip back to kamikaze land.

With one sturdy swoop the extra seat was cleared, and our fly was caught in our trap. The ensign slid gratefully in the only empty seat left in the train. We knew all about maneuvers, and we were all smiles, encouraged by the soldier in the next seat, who produced a bottle of Scotch from his suitcase.

I inhaled deeply. I'm sure I was not the only one who thought, *Women do smell different.* All perfume and scented powder; just to breathe in was a little short of heaven.

Our little wave cutie got off at Pittsburgh, a little worse for wear, but we managed to leave her navy hat in good shape.

I was next off at Philadelphia, where Annie was waiting for me, I hoped. H.P. and Wooten were headed for the Carolinas.

What a welcome at the station. Annie had arrived from Alexandria, and the folks drove over from Wenonah in their Chevy. I zoned in on Annie and gave her a lip lock that threatened to strangle the both of us. Off we drove to Wenonah for a glorious week, which flew by in a wink.

Mother and Dad both worked, so we spent lazy days visiting or cooking dinner for the folks. Our trip to the Bowen family was painful, for we could not believe we would not be seeing Dave again. We went to Camden and had our pictures taken. Ann in her pink wool dress she made for my return, and me in my dress blues, with my ribbons, battle stars and rate on display. One night we went to Streeters nightclub and had our pictures taken there also.

Before I knew it I was back on the train to California and the dry dock where the *Clay* was birthed. Great floodlights covered the ship and the pounding noise of the repair work continued night and day. The troops were not aboard of course, and the landing craft were missing from the decks, so there was plenty of room and water for showers, and not much to do.

I was hoping that Ann could come out, but there was not a room to be found anywhere. If I live to be 100, I will never forget that phone call. I hated to tell her the bad news about no rooms, and when she said hello, I blurted out, "Honey, you just can't come out. I've no place for you to stay."

I was stunned for a moment by her answer. "In the first place, I'm not your honey." A pause. "I'm your mother-in-law. In the second place, your honey left last Friday, and will be arriving Monday at 9 A.M."

"Fri. June 1, 1945 The Home Front and Annie's Traveling Story."

After the first draft call, Washington, D.C. became the hub of all service activity, with the Navy and War Departments worked around the clock. All trains, trucks and buses going north or south passed through Alexandria, Virginia, over the Potomac Bridge to Washington, D.C. Consequently, long trains with troops, trucks, tanks, supplies, and all kinds of armament could be seen passing through at all hours of day and night. Food and clothing rationing was managed by coupons to each family, and gas rationing left no commuter car without every seat filled. Bus transportation was so overloaded that there were long lines waiting, and the crush of service personnel was everywhere. Washington could hardly cope with the influx from the navy, marine and army bases, all within a few hour's distance away. Service branches added to the overcrowding when they imported young girls from all over the country to come to Washington to work for the duration of the war. Rooming houses, apartments, and temporary living quarters were filled with young boarders, away from home and family for the first time. I was fortunate to live with the protection of my family. My mother was widowed, and to pay off her mortgage, the upper rooms were rented to trainer pilots. There were always rooms to clean, and I helped when I was home. On weekends the city was unable to control the foot traffic on sidewalk and streets. Stores and restaurants were packed. Girls and servicemen were everywhere; around the capital and monument grounds, on benches, under the trees, behind the shrubbery, hugging, kissing, crying, talking and some were even fighting. Everyone moved at such a frenzied pace that it was difficult to tell just what was going on. Many times, with great anxiety, I rode the bus from Virginia to the Navy Department, where I had worked since Pearl Harbor. I was an assistant supervisor in the accounting department of the Bureau of Supplies and Accounts. We audited and reconciled naval stock accounts, clothing and small stores transferred between supply officers. This was very important to me because to some extent, I could follow Bill's ship movements, when we audited the supply officer's accounts. We had many girls working in our department who had come from rural areas and big cities, all caught up in the unreality of the moment and all hoping for a great romantic adventure. Marriages happened overnight, and some returned home with unwanted babies, and unwanted husbands. I was greatly concerned with the unfeeling attitude of some girls who openly admitted they were just interested in the transient servicemen for their government allotment. Some caused great heartache for their service husbands overseas, by sending "Dear John" letters asking for a divorce. Thankfully, there were many girls who were very sincere and worked long hours. Ida from Rhode Island and Pepsi the wave yeoman from Wisconsin, joined Bea and I to see a movie and go to dinner once a week. Every day at work was like watching a different kind of movie, and I tried not to get too concerned, but sometimes it could not be helped. One pretty girl in our office, whose husband was overseas, was having a little fling with a young naval officer when her husband came home unexpectedly and found them in bed. The outcome was to be expected. The young officer was badly beaten and she was almost strangled and pushed out of the window, but she was saved by her long talon-like nails that she dug so deep into his face, he was probably scarred for life.

I worked through this turmoil day after day, but as the days, months and years passed by, it seemed there would be no end. When word circulated the office of Bill's ship arriving in San Francisco, friends came forward with addresses of relatives and families in the Oakland area. The Navy was very lenient about leave when husbands were in port, and I had no trouble shifting my workload. If Bill was going to be in California, I was going to be there.

How was I going to travel? There was no gas to drive, too far to go alone anyway. The buses took about ten days and were overburdened with servicemen, but strange events pushed me on my way. On weekends my mother's home was open house to servicemen. I had a cousin based at Fort Belvoir, just south of Alexandria. That weekend he brought Raymond, another distant relative, with him. Raymond had been to our house before for coffee, which they sometimes filched from the mess hall for us, and was just dropping by to say he was shipping out Friday for San Francisco. When I heard his news I said that I was "shipping out" too on

Monday. The end result was obvious, and while he exchanged my ticket, I did a Houdini act with my suitcase. If I do say so myself, I am a good packer, I fold everything the size of my case, which was a little larger than a weekender. I left no spaces for we were only allowed one small carry-on. There was one drawback; it was heavy as lead, but it served me well for I had to sit on it until we reached Baltimore. Raymond was a sergeant major, very tall and slim, and I was fascinated with his red mustache, much redder than his dark red hair. I actually assessed him for the first time realizing I would be in his company for several days and nights and thought with his continental air he would have fit very well into the French Foreign Legion. However, I was on my way to Bill, and that was all that mattered.

Some left the train at Baltimore, and Raymond found us a seat; it was old and hard, but better than the suitcase. All the windows were open wide, and there were servicemen standing and luggage was stacked in every available space; so I couldn't complain. The engine picked up speed and every once in a while a great puff of smoke and soot blew in the open windows. Several tried to close them, but to no avail, so it continued to be a nuisance until Chicago. We were due for a short stop there, for the train to San Francisco would not leave for several hours. I headed straight for the washroom feeling wilted and dirty, but I did not know how dirty until I saw my reflection in the mirror. Horror upon horrors, the trip had just begun, and I looked like the original tar baby. There were black rings around my eyes and nose, and smudges where cinders had caused my eyes to tear. How lucky I was that I wore a black suit; no trouble there, but my new white blouse was smudged and streaked around the collar. With a silent moan for my mother, I could hear her say, "Just check the damage and go on." I took off my blouse and all but took a bath in the sink. Great streaks of dirty water ran down my arms, but I managed to blot it all up somehow. I turned my blouse wrong side out, repaired my makeup and swished my long hair into a ponytail. The trick worked wonders, and I surprised Raymond, who thought I had performed magic.

There were so many servicemen in the station, we could not tell where one line began and where one ended. It looked like they were transferring a whole regiment. We finally got to the boarding gate when a big conductor grabbed me out of the line and said, "Positively no civilians on this run." Raymond got out of the line too, swooped up my suitcase, grabbed me by the arm and stood at the end of another line. This time he went first, and this time there were no questions asked. With my suitcase as a breaker, he pushed his big sergeant major frame ahead and said, "Let my wife by."

This train was more discouraging than the first, if possible. It was the longest train I had ever seen, with two large engines. We walked and walked looking for a seat. Raymond seemed to have a plan as he hurried me from car to car, constantly complaining about the rocks I had in my suitcase. He finally found what he was looking for, an air-conditioned car, but it was jammed packed full except for a double seat with a card on it; "RESERVED FOR MPS." We had seen the MPs on the train platform, and apparently they had not found where their seat was located. No one spoke a word as Raymond removed the card, shoved it under a ventilator, and made a big production out of seating me. Just as I was wishing I could disappear or something, two burley MPs entered the car. Coward that I was, I put my bag on the seat and made a hasty exit for the washroom.

I could hear the conversation as one MP asked if anyone had seen a reserved sign on one of the seats. There was no response, and they moved on. Raymond gave me a big smile and a hug as I eased back into my seat, fully expecting to be exited from the train. He leaned over and whispered, "Remember, you are supposed to be my wife." I knew I was in his debt, but I could not resist telling him that he was really lucky, "Suppose they come back and put you in the brig?" His answer was a little comforting when he told me he would rather be in the brig than where he was going to be sent; besides, rank did have its privileges.

Although it was June, the car was really chilly and my suit did little to keep me warm. All eyes were watching the sarge and his wife as they snuggled under his heavy army jacket. The next two days were spent standing in line to eat; it was beans and franks again, then standing in line for the rest room.

In San Francisco, Raymond said good-bye and kissed me, mustache and all and said, "Thanks for being my wife if only for four days." I felt sad for him, for I knew he did not have a wife to come home to. I never saw him again, and I hope he survived the war, but I will always remember my protective sergeant major with the flaming red mustache.

Bill was excited when he found me on the platform, and could hardly wait to tell me that Kaiser Shipyard had some empty housing, right by the ship and the rent was cheap.

The ship seemed enormous, and the lights and repair activity created quite a din, but we were so glad to be together; nothing could have bothered us. The only tenants in the housing were the wives of the crew, and they were all arriving about the same time. Jo brought along her wedding pictures and had traveled with a girl friend, Ray, from the Philadelphia/New Jersey area. The rooms were large, and there was a community washroom. We had no kitchen facilities, but the local USO gave us cooking privileges once in a while upon request. We were lucky to have a little lunch stand nearby, probably left over from the previous shipyard workers. They had coffee and buns, snacks and a bowl of hard-boiled eggs, which created quite a sensation since the boys had been without eggs for many months. There was a sign over the bowl that read, "One per customer, rationing for our boys overseas." There was an immediate vocal reaction from the boys. The girl smiled and shrugged, but she did give us a few extra ones. We paid our bill, and when we left I noticed the bowl of eggs looked a lot emptier than I originally thought; and I was right. We had barely reached the sidewalk when three eggs bounced on the pavement and rolled on the grass. The boys were grinning, and we couldn't tell who the culprit was, but we made sure they ate them all right then and there. Hard-boiled eggs are mighty dry without a drink, but we had no pity. Living at the Kaiser facility was like a dormitory for all the young wives, and we were in seventh heaven. The girls were a nice group, but the men had been gone a long time and we had to get used to having a stranger in our bed at night. Bill was so brown his teeth fairly gleamed, and so thin he looked like a giant. I was glad that he would be getting food and rest. Phil's wife, Lois, walked right passed her own husband, and was terribly upset when she saw how thin he was. He had lost about 40 pounds from working in the engine room and she had to go to the rest room to control herself. Our boys got passes every night, and liberty on weekends. They seemed to have a lot of nervous energy. Naturally, we had no way of knowing the strain they had been under for the past months.

The first morning we headed out to breakfast and found a little restaurant called The Pirate's Cove. Phil and Lois were in the booth with Bill and I, and all we could do was watch the boys open-mouthed as they devoured a super-sized platter of steak and six eggs, and then ordered another of exactly the same, hardly coming up for air. I was really concerned that they would be sick, especially when they proceeded to finish up what Lois and I could not eat. Far from being sick, Phil was in a singing mood and serenaded us with sea ditties and made up salty poems to the tune of "Ter-ar-a Boom De-A," a serenade we would be hearing many times.

There were about five couples in our group, and we all agreed that we wanted to do all the sightseeing we had time for. We saw Oakland, rented bicycles to ride around Merritt Lake, took the A train, rode the cable cars in San Francisco, ate at the famous restaurant of stars in Chinatown, and at Ocean Beach we all trooped up the hill to Cliff House to view the seals sunning on the rocks. One seal caused quite a sensation by swimming around with a toilet seat on his neck. I wondered if he was putting on an act for tourists or if he could not escape. No trip to San Francisco would be complete without a tour of Nob Hill, and dinner at the Top of the Mark. The Mark Hopkins Hotel was so packed with service personnel we had over an hour wait, but we did not mind. The view was incredible; we could see the Golden Gate Bridge, and the water beyond. Years ago a watchman stood at this spot on Telegraph Hill and signaled the arrival of sailing ships in the harbor.

On the thirteenth of June (my birthday) the girls cooked a spaghetti dinner at the USO, and Jo Tranchina, our resident Italian cook, supervised the rest of us, who had never cooked spaghetti before. This Italian dish was just being introduced to American cuisine, and everyone just ate and ate and ate. Bill gave me a beautiful bouclé purse, which I kept forever. The days flew by and our heavenly days were over. The *Clay* was repaired, and our boys had their work to do. The *Clay* pulled anchor for San Diego, where they would have more maneuvers and testing. Some of the wives took the train home, but Vinnie's wife, Jo, the camera bug and self appointed trip organizer, Ray's wife, and myself, decided to go to San Diego, via Hollywood. Hopefully we would be able to see the boys again before they shipped out for the Pacific.

Lois, Phil's wife, lived in San Diego, and she invited us to stay at her family's home, so we all boarded the train for L.A. Jo, our trip organizer, had a friend who lived in Hollywood; a lovely Chinese actress named Bo Ching. She was married to a stunt man, and graciously invited us to stay at her apartment.

The following day we attended a game show, and had our picture taken in front of Universal Studio. Bo Ching introduced us to a handsome silver haired man, Bill Boyd's stand in, who took us on a tour of his home in Beverly Hills, and Grumman's Chinese theater. We visited the original Brown Derby, and Jo snapped pictures of everything.

San Diego was balmy and warm, in sharp contrast to the cool sea breeze of San Francisco. Lois made us feel at home, and her family found little cottages for us to bunk up in. The boys were on maneuvers in Coronado, and we spent the day there hoping to see them in action. We saw landing craft from other transports beaching and circling, but none from PA 39. When the training exercises were over, they had passes every night, and we were getting used to feeling married again.

We rode bicycles through Balboa Park, and of course since I was small, I got the only bike left … a little one. My vocabulary that day consisted of, "Hey guys wait up for me." The animals were a delight, and we were all floating on clouds. At night we danced at the famous Sherman Dance Hall. It was almost as large as the Steel Pier dance hall at Atlantic City. The photographer took our pictures; Jo and Vinnie, Ray and his wife, Bill and I. We had another record for posterity for July 25, 1945. There was an amusement park near the docking area and we rode on the "largest double Ferris wheel in the world" … never again.

Lois had to go back to work, and we visited her at the Grant Hotel. We were all quite impressed. She was an auxiliary service information guide, and in her perky little military uniform, she was a look-alike for the popular movie star Jean Arthur. We were green with envy, our jobs seemed so colorless, but then we all had our own part in the war effort.

Sailing time approached and the docking area was an ocean of white uniforms and bobbing white caps. The Navy was on the move. It was the last day and we made our way to the Red Sails Café, our arranged meeting place right at the dock. To keep from getting separated in the crunch of humanity, we locked arms as we made our way slowly down the street.

The boys were waiting impatiently, and our good-byes were frantic for there was only a little time left. We now had some idea what had been happening in the Pacific, and could sense great anxiety when they spoke of the kamikazes. I really hated to see Bill feeling so low; he kept saying his luck was sure to run out; the enemy cared nothing for their own lives. Inside a Red Sails match box I wrote "I Love You," and put it in his pocket. There are not enough words to describe the horrible, sinking feeling that strangles the heart, and makes it too painful to face the reality of good-bye.

The ship's horn blew, and the boys resolutely scrambled aboard. We watched in a state of unreality as the ship slowly left the dock. I could not see Bill until he started to frantically wave his white handkerchief back and forth.

What a horrible sick feeling. We watched sadly as the ship faded on the horizon; perhaps for the very last time.

End of Ann's Story

"Fri. July 27, 1945 Left San Diego for Leyte, P.I."

It felt horrible to leave Ann on the dock that way, but I wanted to be with her until the last minute. Unless you have been there, no one knows that sinking feeling of sad hopelessness. However, the open sea has a calming effect, as only a true man of the sea can understand. There is a bond between a sailor, his mates, the captain and his ship that is strong, and somehow you never forget. Although I had a feeling this would be my ship of doom, the love of my country and family welled in my heart, and I knew I must make the sacrifice worthwhile.

The *Clay* was loaded to the gills as usual. We had boarded naval replacements for the fleet, and some one hundred army officers. Also there was a new adjustment to make, a new captain, Ernest M. Eller, USN, had boarded on at San Diego.

We missed the familiar comforting sight of Captain N. B. Van Bergen. He was well remembered for his many trips on deck, his easy smile and the aromatic whiff of his pipe on the sea air. Our captain was the proud holder of the Navy Cross. On January 1942, he was aboard the cruiser *Marblehead* entering the China Sea, when a Japanese bomber made a direct hit.

The ship's hold was an inferno of fire and chemical fumes. Our Captain Van, as we called him, repeatedly rescued his men trapped below deck. The smoke and chemical fumes did much damage to his lungs, and the stress of his transport service and invasions took its toll on his well-being. Pride for our captain was overwhelming. We missed him; he was a true hero who sacrificed his life for his men.

"Sun. Aug. 5, 1945 Eniwetok. Wrote a letter to Ann today. She should be in Alexandria by today."

Wm. C. Stein—USS Clay—Aug. 5, 1945

Dear Ann,

Well, darling, I guess by this time you are home. At least you will be by the time you get this letter. Hope you made it OK and had a nice trip.

I suppose you went as far as Chicago with Jo. I feel much better knowing you didn't have to go alone.

No doubt Mom and George were happy to see you home again. The folks will want to see you too, so try to go up as soon as possible. They'll want to hear all about your trip; the things we did, etc.

Gee, honey, it nearly broke my heart having to see me off that way, but I wouldn't have had it any different for anything in the world. I sure did hate to go, it gets harder every time.

Let's hope it will not have to happen again; that the next time I'll be staying for always.

Anyway, sweetheart, we can be thankful for all the time we had together. It was a lot more than I expected. We had some swell times together; it will be something we will remember always along with all the other good times we have had.

I'll be keeping the little match cover from the Red Sails, I like those three little words very much, and I'm glad you do.

I hope you will be sending those pictures soon. I can hardly wait to see them; especially the ones on Phil's motorcycle.

I guess I'll have to close now, honey, take care of your self, and let me hear from you lots. So long for now. All my love,

Bill

"Mon. Aug. 6, 1945 Hiroshima target for the first atom bomb."

We were underway, about halfway to the Philippines, when the bosun's pipe trilled us to attention. "Now hear this, now hear this, this is your captain speaking. The B-29 *Enola Gay* took off for Tinian August 6, 1945 and dropped an atom bomb over Hiroshima, the headquarters of the Japanese Second Army, at 0915."

At first there was a dead silence, and then as we understood the full meaning of the announcement, we were all jumping and screaming for joy, but soon were called to our battle stations, and we wondered if the Japanese pilots had gotten the word, for they continued to follow and strafe our convoy.

"Thu. Aug. 9, 1945 Nagasaki target for second atom bomb. Russia declares war on Japan."

Three days after the first bomb, on August 9, 1945, the captain made another announcement. "The Japanese have refused any surrender agreement, and a second atom bomb has been dropped on Nagasaki. The Russian government has declared war on Japan."

"Fri. Aug. 10, 1945 Wrote letter to Ann."

USS Clay—August 10, 1945

Dear Annie:

Well, darling, last night I received two letters from you postmarked L.A., then two more from Ogden, and Salt Lake along with your telegram.

I feel a lot better now, knowing for sure that you made it home OK. Not that I did too much worrying, I know that you can take care of yourself, but you know how a person feels about something like that.

I was quite surprised in getting your telegram. In fact I did not expect to be hearing from you so soon at all. Glad you wrote several times on the way home, or I wouldn't have.

Also, today there are two letters from the folks, and one from Aunt Mabel, so it looks like I will be busy answering letters for a while. Mother said she received your telegram saying you are starting home, also that they are both well.

The picture was pretty good; I showed it to Ray a few minutes ago. He got several letters, no pictures though. As yet I have not seen Vinnie, don't know how he made out.

Well, honey, I'm sure glad you had such a nice trip home. You were lucky to get a good coach, and in returning by another route you did get to see a little different scenery, also the cars would be less crowded.

You girls must have had a pretty nice time seeing Hollywood, etc.—you really got around. It looks like you did better than I did; you've seen more places out there than I have anyway. I hope you took a few pictures.

Give me some dope on our bank account and you might know I forgot those socks.

It was swell hearing from you, darling. Take care of yourself. All my love, Bill

Wm. C. Stein MOMM 2/C Navy's Benefit, USS Clay

Author's Note: On this date August 10, 1945, the emperor of Japan tried to intervene, and on August 15, he broadcast surrender to the Japanese people.

"TUES. AUG. 14, 1945 VJ DAY—JAPAN SURRENDERS. THE *CLAY* IN LEYTE GULF. PRESIDENT TRUMAN ANNOUNCED THAT GENERAL DOUGLAS MACARTHUR WOULD BE THE SUPREME COMMANDER OF ALLIED POWERS FOR SURRENDER AND OCCUPATION OF JAPAN."

"SAT. SEPT. 1, 1945 PROCEEDED TO CEBU CITY. LETTER FROM ANN DATED AUG. 15, 1945."

Alexandria, Va.—Aug. 15, 1945

Dear Bill,

Well, VJ Day came yesterday, and we have two days off work. Today I washed all my summer dresses, what a job. Sorry about the pencil. I left my pen at work. Bea and I went to see The Corn Is Green, *and they announced the great news in the movie. When we came out, Washington was in an uproar. I never saw such a celebration. I just had to cry when I thought about you. It took me three hours to get home. I just can't believe it is all over, honey. My head is going around. Honey, I love you so much, it will be heaven to have you home for good. Don't forget that bargain about the baby. Just one year from the time you get home. We will have so much to do.*

Be sure to let me know when you hit the States, so I can arrange to have a week off. How does that sound?

I'm supposed to sing at a wedding Sat., guess I will wear your favorite black lace dress.

The traffic has already picked up, and the gas rationing is off; I hate the traffic on the highway.

Mom is entertaining the boys at the hospital tonight. They play bingo and have eats. I did not go; I guess the amputees will have to miss dancing with me. Ha.

Well, honey, it is late, and I love you and can't wait until you come a knockin' at my door.

Love and Kisses XXXXX(A big red lipstick kiss)

Cebu City lay in complete ruin; from the parts still standing it could be seen that this was once a very beautiful city. We embarked troops, an element of the 182nd Regiment, 1st Cavalry, and headed for Tokyo. We were apprehensive about the extent of our welcome.

"Sun. Sept. 2, 1945 MacArthur signs peace with Japan."

The Battleship *Missouri*, anchored in Tokyo Bay, became the scene of final arrangements of Japanese surrender. The bay was anchorage for 258 warships of all types, representing nations that had been at war with Japan.

Aircraft carriers remained outside the bay, waiting to launch planes to celebrate the official VJ Day.

At 0900 September 2, 1945, the Japanese delegation, looking expressionless, was piped aboard the Mighty Mo, where General MacArthur, Admiral Nimitz, and Admiral Halsey were waiting.

There was a dead silence during the signing until General MacArthur made a short speech. The general, in his dynamic, soft-spoken way with words, extended a mellow and comforting, vocal olive branch for peace.

As the speech ended, 450 carrier aircraft and several hundred Air Force planes gave the formalities a final salute.

As the *Clay* got underway, the bridge announced that Mount Fujiyama, 12,389 feet high, was visible on the horizon. We were still 300 miles away, but we could see its snowy peak. We wondered what condition the harbor would be in.

"SAT. SEPT. 8, 1945 ENTERED TOKYO BAY."

The *Clay* traveled with caution through the swift currents of Tokyo Bay. The minefields were (hopefully) located, but sunken vessels caused difficulty in navigation. The Japanese Battleship *Nagato* lay where it had been bombed. With her pagoda structure half out of the water, she now served as a navigational aid. We anchored near the industrial section; a ghostly, vacant area with structures that extended from Yokohama to Tokyo.

We unloaded our troops and the next day sailed again for Cebu to board occupation troops and for training exercises. All I could think of was, *Doesn't anyone know that the war is over?*

"WED. SEPT. 19, 1945 OTARU, HOKKAIDO, JAPAN."

Today we were issued marine fatigues, jackets and caps, and our amphibious crews were instructed to drain the water from our landing crafts and fill them with anti-freeze. Apparently we were to expect some cold weather, for Russia was just across the channel. We spent the better part of the day boarding the headquarters group of the 307th Regiment of the 77th Division.

That night the temperature dropped, and we were really glad for the heavy fatigue jackets. The waves were soon washing over the decks as we headed north right into a typhoon. When we entered the Tsugaro Straits, the strong currents and riptide again battered our ship and cargo until we entered the harbor. What a graveyard of ships it was. Some were listing, others were half submerged, and many were sitting dangerously on the bottom. We eased our way through with caution, on constant watch for hidden obstacles. This was Otaro and we were the first American ship to enter the port. We proceeded with great anxiety however, apprehensive about being welcomed by a little last-minute revenge. Our submariners had made a successful blockade of the port, and huge mounds of coal (their export) had been stored at dockside for so long, that great weeds had grown through the coal and around the rusty pilings.

The docking area was completely deserted, so we were able to unload our troops and supplies without any interference. We were anxious to get ashore, and Wooten and I got a liberty to tramp through the deserted storehouses and vacant department stores that lined the shopping area. It was a ghost town, no one was in sight, but we forged on looking for something to see or buy. At the very end there was a little building that had a few dusty things on display. The doorway was so low we had to bend our heads to enter and we joked that it must be a town of midgets. The roof was low also, and we had to bend even when we were inside. From somewhere in the back we heard a scraping noise, and two little gnome-like figures emerged with their hands over their heads. With their eyes bulging and teeth chattering, we had to laugh out loud at the horror on their faces. I suppose to them we did look like murderous giants since we were both over six feet tall, muscle thin and dark brown from the tropic sun. I guess we looked even scarier with our bandoliers and K-bar knives in our belt. They kept backing into the corner, holding their necks as though we were going to slit their throats or chop off their heads. It was such a circus we could not stop laughing, and they fell to the floor when I reached in my pocket for some Japanese currency they had given us on the ship. The money attracted their attention. They stood up uncertainly, and I pointed to a few objects; a fan and some chopsticks. I'm sure they had no idea what the bills were worth, but they gave us many pieces of Japanese currency in exchange, which had a picture of an old man with a Santa Claus beard, but instead of a red cap, he had a little black skullcap with a black bow on top. Their numbers were printed like ours, some one's and some ten's. Now I had my Japanese souvenirs, right from Japan, and it was back to the ship to finish our unloading chores. We worked through the night, and by the next evening all the ships were unloaded, and we pulled anchor for Guam.

I gave an inward sigh of relief as we put the port behind us, but at least now I had a sense of closure. I had been a part of the Tokyo Force and knew that now I could go home, knowing I had helped to reach the goal of victory.

We received information that the government had issued a point system for mustering out of the service, and I sure had enough points, but a long way to get home. We were further frustrated when the captain was reluctant to give us a release, and who could blame him, for there were 87 out of 400 rated men who were eligible for release. Our absence would leave their landing craft crews short handed, but we were determined to take the Magic Carpet for home. I had been away for three and a half years. I had seen service in Africa, Sicily, Italy, Saipan, Tinian, Luzon, and the Philippines, ending with Japan, and had eight battle stars to prove it.

The end of hostilities and the unloading at Otaru, Hokkaido, Japan, left me suddenly very tired. The old pain in my back returned with a vengeance, and I had a severe back spasm that landed me in sick bay. This was a terrible state of affairs. We had pressured the captain to release us at Guam, and I was stuck in the infirmary hardly able to move. To make matters worse, the *Clay* was to board marines at Guam for North China. We were given an inducement to remain on the ship to help unload troops and supplies at Tiensin, China, but no advancement in this world would be good enough to keep me on that ship. I just had to get better; well enough to drag my sea bag out of the infirmary to shore.

"Fri. Oct. 12, 1945 Arrived at Guam in late afternoon."

This morning I learned that those with eligible points were to leave the ship at Guam; unlucky me. I had only one night to gather enough grit to drag my sorry back out of sick bay. We had a mail call as soon as we arrived, and a letter from Ann did not cheer me up much, realizing my trip home could be delayed.

Sept. 27, 1945—Night before the fatal step + 3 years

Happy anniversary, how does it feel to carry the ball and chain for 3 years? Still love me?

Darling, I received 2 letters from you tonight; a sweet anniversary gift I'd say. Last week, I received letters numbered 5 &

4. I did not know what it was about but then I received letters numbered 2 & 3. Aunt Mabel sent us a sweet card and a $10.00 check. Mother and Dad sent a cute card and $5.00. I will bank the money, and you can help me use it soon.

I called the folks tonight, and they seemed in good spirits. I joked and talked with them both. After all, we don't have a third anniversary every day. They said they had just been talking about the note you sent them written on a piece of brown paper bag when we were married. That was a big day and the best thing that ever happened to little "Annie." I can live with that little temper of yours, especially when I think of the faults some of my friends have to contend with, drinking and cheating. You are tops, honey, don't think any different. You have always given me everything my little heart desired, and don't think I don't appreciate it. You and your family have done lots for me and I'll always love all of you very much.

I've just had a bath and fixed my hair, have on a new pink nighty and smell sweet as a buttercup, don't you wish you were here? Going up home next weekend and then go to dentist.

I love you, dear,

Ann

"Sun. Oct 14, 1945 Guam; letter from Ann at mail call."

On the back of the envelope, "SWAK" for our third anniversary.

September 28, 1945—11:30 P.M.

Dear Bill:

Well, darling, this was a nice anniversary, but so very sad without you. Well, in the first place George, Mom, Betty and I went to a show. It was Back to Bataan, *boy, was it good! Then we had frozen custard. George gave us $20.00; he said to buy something for our house. That makes $35.00 in gifts. Pretty nice I'd say. I'll bank it until you come home now.*

I've missed you so all day, and I keep thinking about our honeymoon. Gee, honey, it seems like a big dream. I can say one thing, I thank God for the day he gave me such a wonderful husband. When I read those letters you wrote last night, I could have cried.

Again I wish you a happy anniversary, and our toast for tonight is, "May we be in love on our thirteenth as we are on our third." Won't that be a long way off? We will have some happy years in between, though.

All my love, forever and ever,
Ann

It sure was good to have time to write some letters, and the sick bay was quiet.

Sunday October 14, 1945
Guam, USS Clay
Dear Ann,

We arrived here at Guam Fri. I received a few letters. Three from you and one from A. Mabel. There was none at all from Mother and Dad, and none at all yesterday.

Your letters were dated 1, 2, 3 of October. Our old mail hasn't caught up with us yet. Sorry you got all those letters of mine all at one time. They must have piled up somewhere and gone together.

The weather here is pretty warm during the day. The nights are quite cool, though, and at present there is a half moon, so it is pretty. It could be called romantic if there were women to go along with it. There are a number of women on the island, nurses and Red Cross, etc., but of course they are officer's stuff. Not that I give two hoots, of course.

The island itself is fairly nice as far as landscape is concerned, and the color of the water out here is as pretty as I have seen anywhere. As far as getting off here is concerned, we have a pretty good chance. At the present we are just standing by. We have been put on the waiting list at the staging center on the island. We may be called at any time. They told us that the longest someone had to wait here for transportation was 12 days. That's not bad at all. I have my fingers crossed, honey. Things look pretty good, but you never can tell what will happen.

If I do get off here, then it's OK to get the apartment; I'm sure you will do the best thing. Hoping to be back soon, wish me luck, and remember I love you, baby, say hello to everybody.

Love, Bill

"Wed. Oct. 17, 1945 Left the *Clay*."

I was still in sick bay, but a little more comfortable when the orders came through for our release. There was no way I was going to China, so I hoisted my sea bag and struggled to shore, probably doing more damage to my back, which would last the rest of my life. The marine base was newly established on the island as a holding station for their "Magic Carpet" trip home.

Our Base Camp, built by the CB's, was a short distance to the Marine Corps airfield. Our quarters were a small tent city; the sides and floor of each unit were wood, with canvas on the top. Rest was what I needed and the cot felt so good. Drinking water was contained in large lister bags that hung in the streets, and the showers were large tanks of water overhead with a hole in the end and a chain to pull on and off. Each day the water truck came by and filled them up, and it was a treat to get a nice shower and clean up each night. Some mail caught up with us and I finally received an anniversary card from the folks.

September 19, 1945

Dear Son,

Received your letter of Sept. 9, it has been quite a while. Aug. 20 was our last but now we know why. I am glad you are seeing something while you are over there, but just don't trust any of them, they really have been cruel to our boys. Bruce is in Yokohama on the USS St. Paul, *maybe you will see him. Try and keep your courage up, you will get home pretty soon. They are letting them out as fast as they can, but of course they need the Navy yet, so keep a lip upper stiff, as Andy used to say.*

Don't know what to get for your anniversary, only our love and good wishes, but will send Ann some money. It's time to get ready for bed; just finished some ironing, so good night, kid, take care of yourself. May God bless you and keep you safe.

Love, Mother

"THU. OCT. 18, 1945 WROTE A LETTER TO ANN."

Oct. 18, 1945—Guam

Dear Ann,

Well, darling, it is no more Clay *from now on, and no more writing for you. Tuesday night we left the old pig iron son of a so and so behind for the last time in almost two years. (Sweet Irony.) Yes, short stuff, it finally happened, and one of our worries is over.*

The next worry now is when the hell we will get away from here. The usual scuttlebutt is that we will be shoving off soon now, most any day. I imagine that is nearly right, they can't keep us here too long, especially since they are going to lower the point system November 1st. Of course we know nothing definite as usual. We were told to pack and leave the ship in 15 minutes, so we could catch a ship leaving the same day, and then something happened, and we were sent here.

We are living in a tent; just the three of us in this particular one. This is an annex to the receiving station. It is built in a big grove of coconut trees, about 30 miles from the harbor, by the Agano airfield.

Last night here at the base we saw a good show, Over 21, *with Irene Dunn. Tonight the show will be* Unseen, *with Joel McCrea, H. Marshall, and Gail Patrick.*

This place isn't too good, something like Florida, but not as good. Anyway, honey, I have made the first step. I will be home soon if I can get off here in a few days; sure hope so.

Don't write any more, the ship is still in so we will get a few more letters. She is going to N. China. So long, hon, see you I hope, soon. Miss you so much.

Lots of Love,

Bill

W.C. Stein MOMM 2/c, R.S. Navy 926, c/o FPO, San Francisco, Calif.

"Sat. Oct. 20, 1945 Still on Guam."

We had been on Guam eight days now. The CB carpenters built walks and bleachers of sorts where we could watch movies, but the receiving station had some recreational facilities. It is a dusty walk or a short truck ride to the marine air base. The marine pilots were waiting for orders also and offered to ferry us over the island in their C47s. What a ride; those aircraft are profoundly impressive to say the least. There are several ping-pong tables and we passed the time competing in tournaments. I gave Vinnie Tranchina a run for his money, but not much money changed hands.

We woke up one morning to a dire announcement to fall in for a work detail. A bus was waiting to take us to the marine corp base warehouses. We were met by a marine corporal standing by a forklift who pointed at a warehouse full of boxes. "Fall in line, men. These boxes need to be moved," he said. No one moved. After a short silence the corporal turned on his heel in search of the major.

Someone had made a big mistake! After four years, our work details were over, but we all waited patiently until the major appeared. "I understand you refused to fall in for a work detail" he said, more than a little perturbed. "Will the rated man please step forward." Eighty-eight petty officers stepped to the front, and seven or eight chiefs, signalmen, radiomen, etc. "What!" His words exploded in the air. "Aren't these the new replacement recruits?" We informed him in no uncertain terms that we were not, and that four years of work details was enough. They gave us a nice little meal in the mess hall and bused us back to camp. I believe it was the biggest mutiny in history that didn't result in a court martial.

Ann wrote me in her last letter that her anniversary card to me was returned with a note "Return to sender, moved, left no address." If I ever get out of here, I would gladly leave no address. The latest scuttlebutt has it that an APA will be headed for Seattle in about five days, and at this stage I don't care if it is a row boat.

"Wed. Oct. 24, 1945 H.H. Day—heading home."

We were told to board an APA for our homeward trip, and

instructed to pack our sea bags with only bare necessities. No matter how down and dirty I got during the day, I got cleaned up every night when possible, so I made sure I had enough clothes to last me. There was an old school building on shore and we were told to put all our extra things there. In just a matter of minutes, the pile was as high as the roof; mattresses rolled in their hammocks, extra clothing, whites, undress blues, work dungarees, shoes, white navy blankets with USN stenciled on the top, caps, underwear, and any souvenirs that could not be carried.

The ship was packed and with a full load of troops and casualties. I knew there would be little water to wash clothes, and was glad I had saved all my work dungarees. I had saved just enough to last and when my clothes got dirty, I just heaved them over the side and got another set.

San Diego looked like heaven to us but we were unable to land. There was a dock strike and we were sent on our way to Seattle. Didn't they know we wanted to get home? The slow moving APA finally arrived in Seattle about November 4, 1945, and we were destined to spend two more weeks there while the cogs of the US Navy Personnel Separation ground slowly. Needless to say it was rainy with fog every day. We got to see a few movies and joined the other million servicemen to vie for the USO girls at the large dance hall downtown.

November 19 arrived, and we were released to board the *Tennessean* for home. And what do you know, for our grand exit … a Pullman sleeper. Our navy cooks came aboard and did we chow down. It was snowing hard and it was the coldest weather I had ever seen, especially having been in the tropics for so many years. The snow came down in buckets and soon it was piled so high along the tracks we could not see very much; it was like being in a snow tunnel. I had not taken the northern route before, but the cars were cozy with the steam heat from the engine.

The engine traveled slower and slower as the snow kept piling up. Suddenly with a loud clank it stopped entirely to find a large avalanche of snow had covered everything. There was a lot of jerking and banging, and the engine was unhooked to return for help. This was a bad development. Did we survive four years of war to freeze to death, at God only knows where? Without the steam heat from the engine, we very soon became chilled to the bone. We gathered all the coats we could find and kept together in one place, and just when we had about given up hope, a snow engine came and plowed us homeward.

The cooks had been super, cooking us such fantastic meals with steak, mashed potatoes, and real vegetables, so we all got together and emptied our pockets of what cash we had and gave them a lifetime of thanks.

We arrived at the US Naval Personnel Separation Center, Nashville, Tennessee, on November 24, 1945; the great day I had been waiting for had arrived—my honorable discharge from the Navy.

We were given a Thanksgiving dinner with all the trimmings while the navy tailors stitched the Ruptured Duck discharge logo on our dress blues.

With my service ribbons pinned in order, I headed for home. As the train rails clicked, I wondered who had masterminded the tremendous logistics for such a widespread amphibious landing operation. The last amphibious operation at Okinawa had been a giant water exhibition, an exercise in practice, timing and precision; well, we did have a lot of practice.

It is interesting to note that I found an answer to my question while reading Samuel Eliot Morison's, *The Two Ocean War*. Admiral R. Kelly Turner in command planned and trained for this all-encompassing amphibious operation in the Pacific. The units were so large there was no base huge enough to hold them. Men of the Army, Navy and Marines on ships, planes and on the ground, trained alike in timing and precision, with the hope that all would proceed as planned at the time of invasion. Admiral Kelly knew the islands and their atolls. Amphibious maneuvers were based on his two years of island combat experience.

After I returned home in December I received a letter from the

Secretary of the Navy:

The Secretary of the Navy

Washington

December 12, 1945

My dear Mr. Stein:

I have addressed this letter to reach you after all formalities of your separation from active service are completed. I have done so because, without formality but as clearly as I know how to say it, I want the Navy's pride in you, which is my privilege to express, to reach into your civilian life and to remain with you always. You have served in the greatest Navy in the world.

It crushed two enemy fleets at once, receiving their surrenders only four months apart.

It brought our land-based airpower within bombing range of the enemy, and set our ground armies on the beachheads of final victory.

It performed the multitude of tasks necessary to support these military operations.

No other Navy at any time has done so much. For your part in these achievements you deserve to be proud as long as you live. The Nation which you served at a time of crisis will remember you with gratitude.

The best wishes of the Navy go with you into civilian life. Good Luck.

Sincerely yours,

James Forrestal

Mr. William C. Stein, Route 4, Alexandria, Virginia

SERVICE RECORD

North African Occupation
1 star for Sicily
1 star for Salerno
1 Navy Occupation Medal

Asiatic Pacific Area Campaign
1 star for Saipan, Marianas Island June 15, 1944
1 star for Tinian, July 24, 1944
1 star for Leyte, Philippine Islands October 20, 1944
1 star for Lingayen, Luzon Philippines January 9, 1945
1 star for Okinawa April 1, 1945
Asiatic Pacific Ribbon 4 bronze stars
Philippine Liberation 2 bronze stars

In December 1945, Captain Ernest N. Eller was relieved as commanding officer of the USS *Clay*, and our executive officer Archie M. Simonstad took command on December 20, 1945. The *Clay* was decommissioned on May 15, 1946, at the Naval Ship Yard, New York.

On the back inside cover of my *The Ships and Aircraft of the U.S. Fleet,* I listed the transports (work horses) in our immediate convoys and invasions, all with an amphibious crew.

USS *Stanton*	P-69
USS *Barnett*	PA-5
USS *Funston*	PA-89
USS *O'Hara*	PA-90
USS *Procyon*	KA-2
USS *Dickman*	PA-13
USS *Carroll*	PA-28
USS *Betelgeuse*	KA-11
USS *Chase*	PA-26
USS *Lyon*	P-71
USS *Thurston*	P-77
USS *Oberon*	KA-15
USS *Jefferson*	PA-30
USS *Andromeda*	
USS *Arcturus*	
USS *Monrovia*	P-31
USS *Clay*	PA-39
USS *Knox*	PA-46
USS *Middleton*	PA-25
USS *Custer*	PA-40
USS *Sheridan*	PA-51
USS *Wood*	PA-12

The enormity of the naval involvement in WWII was so far reaching it is difficult to explain; however, many ships of war escorted and defended our transports called APAs (Assault Personnel Amphibious).

There were twenty-two transports in our immediate division, and I personally observed and recorded a list of our valiant defenders in action, realistically this list was but a very small part of this tremendous naval armada of ships.

Battleships:
Washington, North Carolina, West Virginia, Maryland, Colorado, California, Tennessee, Pennsylvania, Iowa, New Jersey, South Dakota, Indiana.

Cruisers:
Minneapolis, Indianapolis, Portland, Chester, Salt Lake City, Pensacola, Louisville, Savannah, Honolulu, Boise, Phoenix, Nashville, Philadelphia, Brooklyn, Cleveland, Colombia, Montpelier, Denver, Birmingham.

Destroyers:
Isherwood, Luce, Franks, Pritchett, Bristol, Laffey, Boyle, Champlin, Meade, Murphy, Caldwell, Coghlan, Gillespie, Hobby, Kalk, Laub, McLanahan, Ordronaux, Davison, Glennon, Jeffers, Maddox, Nelson, Baldwin, Earle, Herndon, Shubrick, Beatty, Stockton, Turner, Benson, Mayo, Gleaves, Plunkett, Meredith, Woolsey, Ludlow, Edison, Wilkes, Ingraham, Anderson, Roe, Wainwright, Buck, Mayrant, Trippe, Rhind.

Repair Ships:
Jason, Vulcan.

Destroyer Tenders:
Prairie, Dixie.

Oilers:
Salamonie.

Ammunition Ships:
Rainier.

Cargo Ships:
Almaack, Electra.

Transports from other convoys:
Harry Lee, Neville, Wm. P. Biddle, Fuller, Geo. F. Elliot.

CAPTAIN N.B. VAN BERGEN, USN
COMMANDING
USS *CLAY* APA39
1944

CAPTAIN ROSS A. DIERDORFF, USN
COMMANDING
USS *ELIZABETH C. STANTON* PA69
1943

Navy at Sicily

An American transport unloads off Gela. While little landing boats swirl around, innumerable booms and derricks help lower supplies safely over sides into boats.

USS *ELIZABETH C. STANTON* PA 69
SHIP'S NUMBER PARTIALLY COVRED
WITH PATCH FROM DAMAGE

USS CLAY AFTER DEBARKING TROOPS AND CRAFT.
CARGO NETS AND GANGWAY DOWN. PACIFIC AREA.

MAY 1943—SAILING FOR N. AFRICA.

SEPT. 1943—SALERNO BEACH.

MARCH 1944
EQUATOR
FLIT GUN

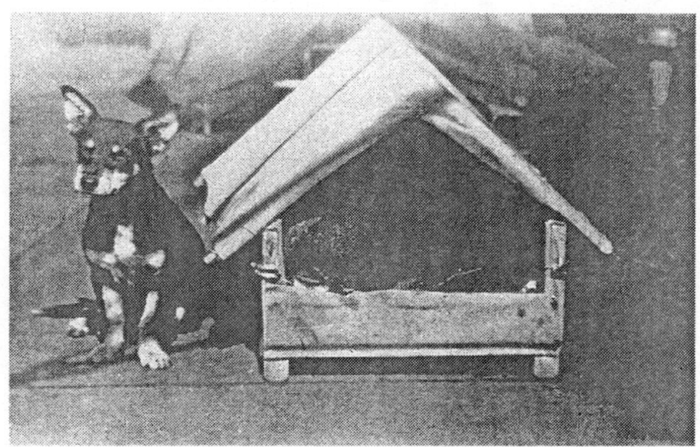

JUNE 1944
SPARKY
FROM SAIPAN

DEC. 25 1944
MANUS

FRENCH USO SHOW—ORAN 1943

ON TO THE PACIFIC—FEB. 1944

H.P. WILSON, COCKSWAIN—HAWAII—BILL STEIN, MACHINIST

PA39—OUR LANDING CRAFT
LEYTE INVASION

ANN & BILL STEIN
WASHINGTON, D.C. 1943

BILL STEIN
FT. PIERCE ATB, FL
1943

ANN & BILL STEIN 1943

BILL STEIN
1943